Springer Series on Cultural Computing

SpringerBriefs on Cultural Computing

SpringerBriefs on Cultural Computing presents concise research in this exciting, emerging field. Designed to complement the Springer Series on Cultural Computing, this Briefs series provides researchers with a forum to publish their cutting-edge research which is not yet ready for a full book in the Springer Series on Cultural Computing but which has grown beyond the level of a workshop paper or journal article.

SpringerBriefs on Cultural Computing are shorter works of 50–125 pages in length, allowing researchers to present focused case studies, summaries and introductions to state-of-the-art research. Characterized by fast, global electronic dissemination, they are subject to the same rigorous reviewing processes applied to the Springer Series on Cultural Computing.

Topics covered may include but are not restricted to:

- Creativity support systems
- Digital communities
- The interactive arts
- Cultural heritage
- Digital museums
- Intercultural collaboration.

SpringerBriefs are published as part of Springer's eBook collection, with millions of users worldwide and are available for individual print and electronic purchase. Features include standard publishing contracts, easy-to-use manuscript preparation and formatting guidelines and expedited production schedules to help aid researchers disseminate their research as quickly and efficiently as possible.

Franziska Baumann

Embodied Human–Computer Interaction in Vocal Music Performance

 Springer

Franziska Baumann
Spiegel bei Bern, Switzerland

ISSN 2195-9056 ISSN 2195-9064 (electronic)
Springer Series on Cultural Computing
ISSN 2661-8710 ISSN 2661-8729 (electronic)
SpringerBriefs on Cultural Computing
ISBN 978-3-031-17984-6 ISBN 978-3-031-17985-3 (eBook)
https://doi.org/10.1007/978-3-031-17985-3

This Springer imprint is published by the registered company Springer Nature Switzerland AG
The registered company address is: Gewerbestrasse 11, 6330 Cham, Switzerland

Dedicated to Daniel, Emanuel, Alisha, Aviv and Sylvia

Acknowledgements

First and foremost, I would like to thank Craig Vear for his invitation to submit a proposal for this book. Without his encouragement, I would not have embarked on this process. His support and helpful comments, and our discussions, greatly helped my work throughout. The process of searching, discarding and refining research and reflection on various aspects related to embodied human–computer interaction in vocal music performance has been instructive and inspiring well beyond this work.

I am grateful to the Springer Cultural Computing series for the contribution of anonymous reviewers, whose detailed feedback helped clarify the book's key concepts and underlying arguments.

The book was largely inspired and shaped by the interviews with singers, composers, artists and researchers Kristin Norderval, Alex Nowitz, Pamela Z. and Atau Tanaka, who generously gave their time, vision and unique insights during the interviews.

Writing a book is a long and extensive process. I see myself as an antenna for ideas and insights that have emerged in the field and that I have learned over the years in many conversations, presentations and performances at concerts, festivals and conferences. In particular, I took much inspiration from the ICLI Symposium in Trondheim in 2020, Kristin Norderval's *VOXLab* Festival in Oslo in 2021 and Alex Nowitz's festival *Designing Voices* in Berlin in 2021, where our music as well as insights were shared in discussions and lectures.

I would also like to thank Bern Academy of The Arts Switzerland. The innovative and progressive field of Composition and Creative Practice at the university provides a flourishing interdisciplinary environment for teaching, research and the exchange of ideas. The collaboration in an earlier research project, "Klang (ohne) Körper"—Sound (without) Body—by Daniel Weissberg and Michael Harenberg provided me with initial research approaches in the field of embodied and disembodied interface performance.

I owe much to my musical and artistic collaborators in the freelance music scene, with whom I have been able to broaden and refine my horizons over the years. In particular, I would like to mention Claudia Brieske, Michel Wintsch, Matthias Ziegler, Christoph Baumann, Angela Bürger and the many great musicians with whom I was privileged to play on my tours. I am also extremely thankful to electronics engineer Andreas Litmanowitsch for the constant development and adaptation of new sensor instruments and his reliable support in case of technical problems. I would like to thank Johannes Schütt from ICST Zurich, with whom I learned to compose with Ambisonic and he was always on hand when there were problems.

Simone von Büren was an invaluable help in finding eloquent English expressions for my thoughts at the beginning of the writing. Tash Siddiqui proofread the final manuscript in a concise time, for which I am very grateful.

Great thanks are also due to the Swiss foundation Landis & Gyr, which honoured me with a six-month artist's grant in London in 2022 and due to the Kanton Bern, which supported the book project with the funding «Förderakzent 2021 Continuer». This gave me the time and space to finish writing this book.

Finally, I reserve my most loving gratitude for my exceptional partner Daniel Repond who has supported my work through all these years with sensor programming, website development, technical support and his generous commitment.

Contents

List of Figures

Chapter 1
Introduction

Abstract This book examines human–computer interaction in live vocal music performance from inside the creative act of music-making. Combined with broad insights into various experiential domains of the contemporary voice, the book builds on and extends the discourse surrounding interactive music systems such as Holland et al. (2019), and conference proceedings such as the ICLI International Conference on Live Interfaces (2020) and the New Instruments for Musical Expression (NIME) research community.

Embodied Human–Computer Interaction in Vocal Music Performance proposes a framework that brings together the embodied and the mediated voice by means of gestural communication through sensor interfaces. When a vocalist performs on stage with technology such as gesture-controlled live electronics, an expanded field of connections between body, gesture and mediated sound is generated. What we see and hear is no longer based on the traditional understanding of sound linked to kinetic energy, such as a violin bow moving across a string. Instead, we are exposed to a holistic experience in which the boundaries between the human voice and the computationally manipulated voice are blurred. Thus, the relations between the voice, the visible gesture and the sound associated with it can no longer be recognised. Far from being a deficit, this offers enormous creative potential for the composition of mapping strategies and the development of an individual *ergomimetic* language for human–computer interaction: "new technologies bring with them practices, ideas and ideologies, and methods and methodologies that enframe how we conceive of the instrument. [...] ergomimetic structures (of acoustic instruments) continue and become implemented in later technical objects" (Magnusson 2019). With digital instruments, the gesture of bowing no longer necessarily results in a bowed sound. By selecting unique gestures assigned to sonic imagination, vocal artists define an embodied practice that is freed from traditional instruments.

While there is much research on motion capture and gesture sound-mapping techniques, less is known about how performers and especially vocalists interact with gestural interfaces and the skills required to achieve nuanced and subtle control of existing or adapted systems. Many analyses of performers' movements have so far focused on functional aspects, providing definitions of sound-producing gestures responsible for expressivity, excitement and modulation. Since, in the case of a singer on stage, physical expression is equally co-responsible for understanding the performance, the gesture interface is situated in a closer understanding of the body. The singer's body itself is a source of sound, and the gestures not only change the perception of sounds conveyed by the digital interface, but also the vocal sounds produced in the body itself.

This book aims to situate and contextualise various aspects that generate meaningful connections in interface performance practice for vocalists. It offers a framework for understanding such creative practices between humans and computers in gestural live music performance, from the perspective of the embodied relationships (i.e., operating inside) within such systems. It examines the potential of the contemporary voice within mediated practices and underlying practices, principles and sensor technologies that support creativity in embodied human–computer interaction in music performance. It presents a dynamic framework and tools for anyone wishing to engage with this subject in depth.

After more than 20 years of practice-oriented research in the field of contemporary vocal performance, electroacoustic composition and sensory live-electronic interfaces in multichannel vocal performance with concerts and presentations around the globe, I (the author Franziska Baumann) present a creative framework for the dynamic interaction between mapping strategies and potentials of meaning. My research considers human–computer interaction less from a purely technical point of view than from a phenomenological and aesthetic perspective, in which gesture, body and the appearance of the interface generate meaning in live music. This expansion of the vocabulary and the practical possibilities for embodied human–computer interaction presented in this book constitutes a valuable resource not only for musicians, composers and researchers but also for human–robotic researchers, voice-based robotic and companion bots and creative practitioners in the fields of creative computing, new instruments for musical expression as well as for actors and dramaturgs in musical contexts.

1.1   Diving Deeper into Embodied Human–Computer Interaction

The general practice of human–computer interaction in music performance involves musicians and performers using interfaces as controllers to support the music they want to make (Baalman 2020). Musicians design their performative interfaces in such a way that they can control their technical functions. In these scenarios, the level of the embodied communication of music with digital interfaces is therefore negligible. For example, a DJ may use a control interface to manipulate sound in real-time and to trigger loops and tracks for live mixing. How he moves doesn't necessarily communicate the sounding result. This example involves functional design considerations based on how best to deliver the music one wishes to produce. Since, in the case of a singer on stage, physical expression is equally co-responsible for understanding the performance, the gesture interface is situated in a closer understanding of the body. The singer's body itself is a source of sound and the gestures not only change the perception of sounds conveyed by the digital interface, but also the vocal sounds produced in the body itself.

Gestural systems of this nature, therefore, open up the potential to interact with digital interfaces in such a way that movements can be individually shaped and designed. Musicians can create expressive nuances that are often lost in conventional applications with knobs and buttons. For live electronic performers seeking broader expressive possibilities, gestural interfaces offer the ability to incorporate extended movement and control. They can investigate gestural systems to develop their individual movement vocabulary and imprint their unique body signature on a live vocal performance. Establishing meaningful and coherent connections in gestural systems remains an ongoing challenge for vocalists seeking to translate nuances of the human movement into sonic processes. To promote meaningful experiences, it may be of great benefit to understand not only the functionality but also the dynamic of the vocalist's body as the re-embodiment of the mediated voice through gestural interface communication. Observation and analysis of body sensations and body feelings can help to design satisfactory gestural systems and define socially acceptable gestures in movement-based interaction (Fig. 1.1).

As Fischer-Lichte argues in her seminal study *The Transformative Power of Performances*, any performance ("Aufführung") is perceived as a "listening space"

Fig. 1.1 Franziska Baumann performing at Jazzfestival Schaffhausen, Switzerland 2007. *Source* © Francesca Pfeffer

("Hör-raum"), a "theatron" ("Schau-raum"), while at the same time being a space of embodiment (Fischer-Lichte 2008). When a performer improvises or plays a composition using sensors, he or she communicates the musical idea through a combination of visible "biosignals" and the resulting sounds. Therefore, perceiving a performance and its meaning offers an embodied experience not only as listener but also as a viewer. In contrast, if we see someone sitting at a laptop playing complex music with a poker face, we cannot tell whether they are making music or writing emails. In this case, the use of technology in the interaction between the generated music and the depicted control functions involving gestures is negligible, so we lack—or lessen—a fundamental condition of conveying and therefore perceiving meaning. This perspective is critical if we are to understand the type of meaningful relationships created between performing musicians and their computer collaborators as defined by this book. Michel Waisvisz, a pioneer in the field of gesturally controlled music, states:

> The algorithm for the translation of sensor data into music control data is a major artistic area; the definition of these relationships is part of the composition of a piece. Here is where one defines the expression field for the performer, which is of great influence on how the piece will be perceived (Waisvisz 1999).

To build meaningful relationships, we may need to understand musicians' underlying practices and their artistic motivation for using "the algorithms of translation".

1.2   New Interfaces = New Relationships

With gestural systems, the artist has to make decisions about the gestural design. As users of existing tools, we have to deal with their traditional logic and idiosyncrasies. The signal flow of sensors in an analogue-to-digital interface is always the same, but the corresponding gestures can be individually adapted. Musicians use sensors to build body-related instruments such as gloves, wearable hand instruments, finger rings and standalone sensor objects. In contrast to a traditional instrument, we use them to build our ergonomics individually. How we play them then designs an organology (Magnusson 2019), and in an ergomimetic game, we invent new body sound images. While the technology involved keeps changing, the questions of its appearance and its interrelationships within the embodied interface performance can remain the same and be transferred to new technologies. Reflection on vocalists' embodied vocabulary for gestural systems may therefore help to understand ergomimetic principles, regardless of the different types of hardware and software they use. Therefore:

> **I aim to explore the question of body presence and interface appearance and to ask about phenomenological aspects in gesture composition and the meaning-making potential of the mapping strategies.**[1]

---

[1] Mapping strategies are the programmed allocation of gestures to sound level.

To this end, I will involve three other vocalists and a musician from the experiential domain of embodied musical interaction with sensor interfaces. These performers and composers interviewed for this book reflect the early implementers of sensor-based technology in live music performance and their long-term engagement with gestural systems on performer agency and identity. I will incorporate quotes from interviews I conducted online in 2021 and live in 2022. The complete interviews are available online.[2]

Pamela Z is an American composer, performer and media artist best known for her solo works for voice with electronic processing. Her performances combine various vocal sounds, including bel canto opera, extended experimental techniques and spoken word, with samples and sounds created by manipulating found objects. Z's musical aesthetic is one of sound accumulation. She usually manipulates her voice in real-time using the software Max on a MacBook Pro to overlay, loop and alter her live vocal sound. Her performances include a wireless sensor instrument attached to her hand and a standalone sensor instrument.

Alex Nowitz is a Berlin-based vocalist–composer. His invention, the *Strophonion*, is an instrument reminiscent of Michel Waisfisz's "The Hands", developed at STEIM Amsterdam. The Strophonion provides buttons for changing functionality and playing different pitches and various types of sensors to measure movements of hands and arms. The data thus obtained is processed and translated into sonic and musical parameters.

Oslo-based singer and composer Kristin Norderval plays with two wireless Wave Rings by Genki, i.e. rings that can be put on like jewellery. Her goal is to use the wireless sensor instruments so that she does not need visual feedback on the computer.

In addition to the three vocalists from the experiential field of embodied musical interaction with sensor interfaces, I will incorporate quotes from an interview I conducted with Atau Tanaka at Goldsmiths, University of London. Tanaka's compositions feature no external sensor object, but draw on internal physiological muscle-sensing data. By tensing his arms and making concentrated gestures, he sculpts sound coming from the computer by shaping and modulating parameters of sound synthesis and sampling. The similarity with gestural sensor systems is that the muscle-sensing data also reacts in relation to the body and not to three-dimensional space as in a motion detection system. All these musicians have a deeply rooted physical practice with gestural systems. Their insights are of great value to situate and contextualise various perspectives at the intersection of human–computer interaction and gestural computer music performance.

---

[2] The quotes from the interviews used in the book can be read in full here: http://www.franziskabau mann.ch/en/press/

1.3 What is in the Book

The three chapters of the book are dedicated to practical experience and how aspects of meaning are generated through the phenomenological and technical intersection of body, gesture and mediated sound. By discussing experiences from my own artistic research and practice and in dialogue with the vocalists and researchers from the experiential domain, I present various insights and frameworks based on such reflections.

In the first chapter, we see that "The Embodied Voice" or acoustic voice is represented by a *multivocal* approach. Beginning with the Dada movement and followed especially by the American female vocal performers of the late 1960s, the so-called non-idiomatic voice has achieved a broad artistic acknowledgment. Vocal performers of the first hour like Meredith Monk, Laurie Anderson, Diamanda Galas and others have inspired the following generations with their individual approaches to vocal performance.

The *multivocal voice* goes beyond defining the voice in conventional terms with related extended techniques, because it no longer takes the western European way of singing as standard. The extended use of the voice, western bel canto, vocal utterances and stylistic and ethnic colours are considered equal. Based on listening aspects developed by Denis Smalley and Pierre Schaefer, I propose an approach in which all vocal expressions in their musicalisation are on the same hierarchical level. It is an evolutionary step towards a new posthuman understanding of the voice in contemporary vocal arts practice.

Chapter 2, "The Mediated Voice" unfolds a radical vocality (Verstraete 2011) separately from the body where the 1st person becomes a 3rd person or where the "I" becomes a "From Me" (Norderval 2020). It draws upon images from abstract vocal terrain, myths as well as everyday disembodied voices such as speech assistants and telephones, and it conjures up imaginary bodies for the disembodied voices surrounding us. In this chapter, the discussion is opened up into a dialogue with other practitioners of the experiential domain. Based on interviews, artistic perspectives on the subject of embodied human–computer interaction, and discussions of the way meaning is generated within their human–computer interactions, are presented. The interviews focus on the practitioners' aesthetic motivation and on how they phenomenologically implement their individual aesthetic with their technology. What are the qualities of their gestures assigned to sound, what is their experience with embodiment and voice, what role do their props play? The answers serve as the starting point for the categorisation of qualities of interactions between bodily movement and electronic sound.

The third chapter invites the reader to discover ways to compose and compile mapping strategies that encourage creativity in the embodied interaction between humans and computers. Several perspectives of gestural communication between the embodied and the disembodied voice through sensor interfaces are presented between the "I", the "From Me" and "Clones of Myself". Visible aspects like gender, dress, wearables and interface appearance affect the impression of the sonic aesthetic.

Together with the involved gesture vocabulary and the resulting sound, a feedback loop of embodied perception is created which constantly reorganises what we see and what we hear in our perception.

The three chapters serve as a particular lens of embodiment through which to look at types of music using human–computer interaction. They aim to give a deeper understanding of how meaning is generated in human–computer interaction by the mutually constituent domains of voice, body, gesture and disembodied sound. By bridging the gap between technology and phenomenological aspects, important insights can be gained that will be of interest to artists, musicologists, software developers and even actors and dramaturgs.

References

Baalman M (2020) Mapping the question of mapping. In: Proceedings of the 5th international conference on live interfaces. Norwegian University of Science and Technology, Trondheim, Norway. https://www.researchcatalogue.net/view/908792/908793. Accessed 8 Aug 2022

Fischer-Lichte E (2008) The transformative power of performances: a new aesthetic. Routledge, London

Magnusson T (2019) Sonic writing, technologies of material, symbolic and signal inscriptions. Bloomsbury Academic, New York

Verstraete P (2011) Vocal extensions, disembodied voices in contemporary music theatre and performance. https://www.academia.edu/3035586/Vocal_Extensions_Disembodied_Voices_in_Contemporary_Music_Theatre_and_Performance. Accessed 8 Aug 2022

Waisvisz M (1999) Gestural round table. In: Wanderley MM, Marc B (2000) Trends in gestural control of music. Paris. DVD. http://www-new.idmil.org/project/trends-in-gestural-control-of-music/. Accessed 9 Aug 2022

Full Interviews

Norderval K (2020) Interview. http://www.franziskabaumann.ch/en/press/interview3-norderval.php. Accessed Aug 2022.

Nowitz A (2021) Interview. http://www.franziskabaumann.ch/en/press/interview2-nowitz.php. Accessed 12 Aug 2022

Pamela Z (2021) Interview. http://www.franziskabaumann.ch/en/press/interview1-pamela.php. Accessed Aug 2022

Tanaka A (2022) Interview. http://www.franziskabaumann.ch/en/press/interview4-nowitz.php. Accessed Aug 2022

Chapter 2
The Embodied Voice

Abstract In this chapter, I introduce how listening to the purely sonic properties of vocal sound transforms our understanding of the voice's musical meaning. I present the listener with the *multivocal voice*, a perspective that goes beyond the established western European tradition and considers a new type of musical orientation in contemporary vocal art. The first section discusses the nature of the term *multivocal voice*. It gives a brief historical outline of how contemporary vocal arts practice has roots in vocal performance art, initiated by women in the USA in the sixties and seventies. I argue that the multivocal voice represents a communication platform beyond cultural idioms. The following section analyses how the sonic properties of the human voice become an instrument for music-making. I apply the concept of Denis Smalley's *spectramorphology* and Schaeffer's *listening modes* to outline extrinsic and intrinsic vocal qualities. The final section explains how *radical vocality* helps us to understand the creative potential of the abstract vocal terrain as a precondition for the mediated voice.

2.1 Introduction

Among musical instruments, the voice is a special case. It constitutes our most embodied instrument; it is an instrument without an external device. The voice as a performative phenomenon connects different and partly contradictory intrinsic and extrinsic spheres; it is simultaneously inside us and outside us. Doris Kolesch and Sybille Krämer (Kolesch/Krämer 2006) define the voice as a "threshold phenomenon"[1] or as a paradigmatic figure of transgression. It is both body and spirit, or body and "symbolic order". The many ways we hear voice are based on a trained human communication process, deep emotionality and cultural context.

From a physical perspective, the embodied voice is always two things at once: a vibration through the body and the effect of that vibration outside the body. Musical instruments are devices used as a mediated extension of the body. An instrumentalist

---

[1] Translation of the German word "Schwellenphänomen".

has an instrument, and vocalists are the instrument; one in which the body acts as a resonating instrument, as an interface of the voice.

A significant difference between vocal and instrumental materiality is that the voice connects the person and the body with emotion, meaning and communication. The sound creation of a vocalist is intimately connected to the person. People who are not used to singing feel naked when they have to sing in front of others. It can feel like exposing yourself without protection. When people come together to sing, it is not only their sound that connects but also their emotions and bodies. The voice thus references the person through its vibrating presence both outside in space and inside the body.

Alex Nowitz has defined the term *multivocal voice*, which includes multiple, diverse singing and vocal techniques, and linguistic and everyday utterances. It extends what he calls the *one register voice* from the eurocentric listening habit and includes all singing, speaking and extended vocal expressions (Nowitz 2019). It welcomes the ever-changing and vast landscape of diverse vocality that is at our disposal. Through the variety and crispness of vocal sounds produced, the aim is to achieve a deepened aural awareness and focused consciousness that endows both performer and listener with an openness of far-reaching quality.

Going even further, we can apply musical thinking to all vocal utterances, expressions, speaking voice and singing techniques. If we treat vocal utterances musically in similar ways, we try to shift the attention towards the purely sonic properties of the vocal sound. In this way of listening, the extrinsic threads of the symbolic order, trained communicative processes, emotionality and cultural context become secondary. I will link this idea to the concepts of spectromorphological (Smalley 1997) and reduced listening (Schaeffer 1966). It reveals a practice that goes beyond the traditional interpretation of vocal events into multiperspective listening through enhanced listening attitudes. As a pure vocality beyond any socialisation, it may offer transcultural links between individuals, so they understand each other on a different level. It is a communication platform for discovering, activating, remembering, uncovering and revealing new aesthetic experiences. The creative potentials of spectromorphological and reduced listening concern musicalising a *radical vocality* (Verstraete 2011). It helps us to understand the creative potential of the abstract vocal terrain as a precondition for the mediated voice which I will then explore in this chapter.

Before I go into the intrinsic and extrinsic qualities of the embodied voice in depth, I would like to offer a brief historical outline of vocal performance in recent decades. Without claiming to be complete, I highlight the work of some female vocal performers that has led to the contemporary movements in vocal music performance and who have also been significant inspirations for my work. The vocal and performative work of these pioneers is a crucial prerequisite for understanding the embodied and disembodied voice in human–computer interaction.

2.1.1 The History of the Multivocal Voice

In recent decades, the interest in extended vocal practices has significantly increased. Vocal improvisers and composers no longer take the western ideal of the one-register voice as the standard. As Alex Nowitz (2019) describes in his Ph.D., *multivocality* takes into account different forms of virtuosity in terms of methods, be it the experimental voice, various singing techniques, ethnic vocal sounds, speaking voice, and human vocal expressions. It displays a posthuman ideal in which the one-register voice is no longer at the centre with extended techniques on the periphery, but in which diverse vocal manifestations are expressed at the same hierarchical level (Fig. 2.1).

Alex Nowitz explains in the Zoom interview:

> Concerning singing techniques, we have a set of possibilities at our disposal. The range becomes almost unlimited if you merge those with speaking and extended vocal techniques. You were, anyways, coming back to your question about the discourse of posthuman systems theories. What they do is often proclaim a "new materialism". This is, in fact, at the core of the concept of the "multivocal voice" that is, to come up with new sounds and new sound assemblages. (Nowitz 2021)

Theda Weber-Lucks (2008) speaks of the inclusion of "all the sounds and tones of the different languages, vocal styles and noises of the world" (translated by the author).

This approach to contemporary vocal arts practice has its roots in vocal performance art. This type of vocal arts practice was initiated by women in the USA in the sixties and seventies. Among the pioneers are composer–performers Meredith Monk, Joan La Barbara, Diamanda Galás, Pauline Oliveros, Laurie Anderson, and, in the second generation in the eighties, Pamela Z and Shelley Hirsch. An initial role model was possibly the vocalist Cathy Berberian, who lived in Italy but grew up in the USA. Her artistic path of exploring her own voice and its possibilities went far beyond the bel canto sanctioned in the "modern West".

In the sixties, Fluxus and Happening, and the early vocal experimental avant-garde of sound poetry, experimental theatre, new vocal music and Free Jazz opened up a new understanding of body and voice. In the late sixties and seventies, New York "Downtown" was the boiling centre of a counter-cultural, avant-garde arts scene. An

Fig. 2.1 Zoom interview in May 2021: Alex Nowitz in Berlin and Franziska Baumann in Berne. *Source* © Franziska Baumann

essential feature of this cultural downtown was the development of new art forms and decidedly individualistic artistic practices. The highly individualistic use of specific techniques tailored to one's abilities and preferences, resulting in an idiosyncratic use of voice and individual vocal style, is a characteristic of vocal performance art. This is also closely linked to the composer–performer criterion: the vocalists perform their music themselves, based on experiments, possibilities and experiences with their own voice.

An essential feature in vocal performance art is the amalgamation of different functions within one and the same artist in the sense of a "VocalComposerPer-former" (Weber-Lucks 2008). The prerequisite for being able to individually shape and expand one's own vocal and stylistic repertoire is the transgression of, or the detachment from, one-dimensional conventions and traditions as well as the expansion of possible points of reference and influences that are characteristic of singing in the twentieth century.

Meredith Monk has developed a distinctive non-verbal vocal language in which she combines timbre and emotional expression in a rhythmically complex way (Monk 1997). Over time, her melodies, harmonies and vocal techniques have again and again been associated with non-western musical traditions or historical vocal styles or traditions outside of western art songs. She maintains, however, that she generates all sounds from experimenting with her own voice and negates any reference to external musical influences.

Influenced by these body-voice trends, Joan La Barbara began to explore her voice in the early seventies and understands the voice as an "original instrument" and "guide into the realm of the unconscious" (La Barbara 1976). By creating new situations of self-awareness in the framework of partly stringently designed laboratory experiments, she challenged herself to spontaneous vocal expressions (Kohl 2015). Also, in the mid-seventies, singer, pianist and performer Diamanda Galás discovered and explored her body voice as a combatant, weapon and shield, creating her emotionally charged, ecstatic performance style by exploring the art of the scream. Laurie Anderson's splitting her voice into a male and a female voice provided an irritatingly ambiguous play on established concepts of gender difference and androgyny (Oehlschlägel 1984).

The distinctive artistic personalities of these early female vocal performers shaped the way they researched, experimented and composed with the voice. This gave rise to a unique kind of vocal performance art in which they performed simultaneously as composers and interpreters of their music. Through their strong international impact in the 1970s, these women artists established the essential characteristics of vocal performance art as an independent musical genre. Such characteristics include an individual, non-verbal vocal style, extended vocal techniques, a concert or staged performance art style and the realisation of a performance.

Voice experiments that seek to go beyond the boundaries of what has so far been known and perceived as vocal art have mostly been the domain of women. It may be that women have found it easier to assert themselves in areas that have not been mainly dominated by men. Also, in terms of aesthetic and cultural history, artists in the USA were less burdened with historical references than those in Europe. These may have been important reasons why American women could establish themselves in the new field of vocal performance art and define their individualistic vocal art form.

Vocal performance art has also expanded outside the USA. Many of the emerging European vocal artists in the eighties and nineties were influenced by American vocal performers such as Joan La Barbara or Diamanda Galás, who had been coming to Europe for festivals since the late sixties. Also, the vocalists Shelley Hirsch and David Moss have provided essential stimuli to experimental vocal music in Europe and have had essential exchanges with the European scene as artists holding a DAAD[2] scholarship in Berlin.

European vocalists such as Maggie Nicols, Lauren Newton, Demetrio Stratos, Phil Minton established themselves as experimental vocalists between Free Jazz, free improvisation, new music, sound poetry and vocal performance art. Later in the nineties and in the dawning twenty-first century, a third generation of vocal performance characters like Ute Wassermann, Isabelle Duthoit, Maja Ratkje, Audrey Chen, Alex Nowitz and myself turned up in Europe, to name but a few.

The range of improvised and composed contemporary vocal practice has opened up a wide variety of cultural references and aesthetics. It uses the sounds and tones of the various languages, vocal styles and sounds of the world and incorporates elements from the performative arts of dance, theatre and music. It is close to all the forms of experimental vocal art that emerged from the early avant-garde movements.

As for my own development, I had an artist's residency in New York for a couple of months in the mid-nineties. I experienced new possibilities of how music could be listened to and discussed. Free from the compartmentalised thinking of the "European super fathers", for me, this opened up artistic perspectives that went far beyond conventional categories.

My work was reflected differently than in Europe, the focus was less on the extrinsic qualities of the cultural context than on the intrinsic qualities of the individualistic use of the voice, compositional techniques, and live electronic processing. It was a formative time for me, in which I learned to no longer view my own approach in comparison with traditional styles but as an art form in its own right. The culturally vibrant environment in New York provided me with the necessary background to develop and expand my own vocal technical and stylistic repertoire in an autonomous and individualistic way and to detach myself from the classical western conventions and traditions that had shaped composition as well as singing techniques and styles in the 20th century.

I have always been interested in working with unique voices full of character. The hermetic technical and idiomatic approach to academic and standardised voices used to be rather suspicious to me and less interesting from the aesthetic standpoint. My experience with bel canto arias, yodelling as well as jazz songs

---

[2] The German Academic Exchange Service (Deutscher Akademischer Austauschdienst).

mainly served as a basis to explore timbres, which I then used in my own compositions. Although I refer to traditions and concepts of jazz, composed and improvised music in my works, the aim of the sound spaces I create is not a historical forensic quest but a sensual exploration of the most diverse possibilities of contemporary music making. In my improvisations and compositions, I have also been attracted to exploring the everyday voice with its infinite facets of colour, the rough, the pale, the subtle, the shouted, the casually said, the colourfulness of the voices of passers-by in different languages, the voices of my siblings on the farm calling things to each other across the distance. I have been fascinated with shaping and musicalising the fragile, unembellished spellbinding timbres, sudden outbursts, laughter and sighing, and clearing of throats and groans on the edge of sound.

A further method of generating new vocal material has been the translation of non-human environmental sounds into vocal phenomena. For example, the cargo trains shunted on the tracks at night at the railway station next to the house I used to live in. Trying to find an adequate vocal phenomenon for this intriguing track sound I came up with a very high fluttering voice and multiphonics.[3] I generally focus on the materiality of the sound, not only as an exercise at home but also when improvising on stage. I follow a particular sound and attempt to play with these specific particles of the sound spectrum and try out what is possible. How low can I go on the sound spectrum, how high, how loud etc.? Or can I set rhythmic accents that interact with a drummer? That's where the composer's ear is at work. As vocalists nowadays we benefit from a broad range of vocal research as well as increasing physiological research and findings. An excessive vocal terrain unfolds through a range of vocal practices that oscillate between poles of aesthetics influenced by Dada, various singing, belting, and yodelling techniques, between vocal phenomena outside music and intrinsic experimentations that reveal the pure sound as such and vocal morphologies derived from the computer manipulation of vocal material. Throat bass and whistle registers, noisy articulations without definable register, multiphonics, harmonics, glottal beats in all variations, screams, grunts, gasps, and shouts are part of a hybrid approach that joins idiomatic vocal techniques on an equal level.

Vocal techniques are usually tailored to the individual's articulatory and vocal possibilities and are often difficult to transfer from one artist to another. However, they can be a source of inspiration for one's journey of discovery. If we try to imitate, a lot of interesting outcomes may be generated.

These new vocal approaches both inspire and demand different ways of listening and reception. Most people are not used to listening to familiar vocal sounds such as grunts, creaks, howls and shouts as musical components. Furthermore, experiments

---

[3] Listening example: Rumors on nonclassical London UK (2020) https://nonclassical.bandcamp.com/track/rumors.

such as vibrating the pocket folds in the larynx or playing with vocal harmonics and multiphonics tend to be associated with non-European or ethnic singing. When we experiment with our voices, we may end up using vocal techniques reminiscent of a particular musical tradition. However, in our compositions, they may not be meant to refer to those traditions but are the result of our very individual explorations. By considering these explorations as abstract vocal phenomena, we may create an apparent conflict between cultural codes and new ways of listening to and composing with such sounds. This conflict can be perceived both as a friction and—on a meta-level—a communication that goes beyond cultural idioms. Alex Nowitz says that there is a vision involved:

> How can we understand each other? I believe human beings, no matter where they come from, no matter what cultural background they have, can easily understand each other. I see it as a communication platform that hasn't been explored enough yet. As vocal specialists, we might understand each other in a broader sense (Nowitz 2021).

The above conflict between the extrinsic and intrinsic qualities[4] of familiar or seemingly ethnic-sounding vocalities can be resolved by a precise listening virtuosity, as a basis for further musical processing, as will be elaborated below. If we can detach ourselves from the given context of the vocal sound and think it anew, creative forces are released, and imaginative freedom for compositions and improvisations can be increased. It requires the courage to accept vocal events in their nakedness and to immediately switch to a level of innocence in listening and apply the "composer's ear" to it. If we improvise we have to shift our attention quickly between several levels of perception. As Alex Nowitz says:

> During an improvisation piece, I discover an unusual sound that interests me. I try to focus on and follow it, playing with its essential components and exploring its potential. At this moment, it is the composer who's at work. To me, improvisation is a method of instant composition. Usually, the composer has plenty of time to think about and probe various approaches and possibilities until the final composition is completed and done (Nowitz 2021).

In the following sections, I propose to listen to the nakedness and immediacy of the voice in its pure materiality. By decoupling vocal expressions from familiar psychological associations, we can shape and compose the vocal material in a purely sonic approach and thus open up new creative and aesthetic experiences. This requires active listening since the emerging psychological content in the new vocal approach is not fixed and transmitted by the performer directly. Rather, the musicalisation of the original expressions opens up a field of multiple possible meanings and offers a new aesthetic experience to the listeners.

Maybe an example from the fine arts helps to illustrate the point: Swiss sculptor Jean Tinguely[5] decouples the original functions from mechanical parts of machines in order to create new visionary mechanisms without economical functions. What

---

[4] The intrinsic and extrinsic aspects of music are discussed fully in Nattiez 1990: 102–29.

[5] Jean Tinguely (1925–1991) was a Swiss sculptor best known for his kinetic art sculptural machines that extended the Dada tradition into the later part of the twentieth century.

makes these machine sculptures so fascinating is the fact that as viewers we inevitably tend to attribute new particular purposes or functions to them. In a similar way, listeners to vocal performance may automatically assign new meaning to vocal sounds which have been decoupled from any particular symbolic meaning and musicalised by the vocal artist.[6]

2.1.2 The Human Voice as an Instrument

Giovanni Piana (1998) reminds us in his *Philosophy of Music* that "singing is nothing but the echo of a cry". With this in mind, this section examines the voice in the first instance as an instrument that requires a distance to enable a de-subjectivation and to free its sound from the "human in the voice". This allows wider dimensions of listening: the voice in the echo is a voice without subject, an impersonal voice, no longer an individual voice, but a sound that we listen to. It is the precondition for establishing what I call "virtuoso listening" (Hörvirtuosität). This is not to say that the body as a source is no longer relevant. The listener cannot merely brush aside what I call "psychological listening", which is linked to a culturally conditioned and mostly unconscious process. Psychological listening refers to the human expression, to emotionality and images associated with the vocal sound, rather than the pure sonic qualities themselves. For example, a sung "ah" sound can be perceived as sighing or moaning rather than a vowel with a considerable amount of breath at a particular pitch. Thereby, psychological listening can at times even obscure the musical meaning. As Don Ihde says: The first movement of phenomenology of sound and listening moved from the listening to the voices of things "outward". [...] There is primary listening to the voices and things of the World. [...] Listening comes before speaking (Ihde 2007).

We listen to things and messages. It is not easy to evolve a purer "instrumental" ear that is unaffected by psychological listening in the face of so many psychological concerns that may disturb the creative flow and cloud the perceptual judgement. Shifting away from the familiar and taken-for-granted paradigm of listening and at the same time focusing on a specific listening sensation may enable us to take note of what is usually overheard. If I use the moaned "ah" rhythmically in an improvisation, it can become an exciting vocal colour. I may change pitch and vowel and vary the colour with varying glottal pressure. It thus can give us a fresh sense of the experience of the moment.

Denis Smalley proposes the development of a "purer" spectromorphological ear:

> Spectromorphological thinking is based on criteria which can potentially be apprehended by all listeners cutting across national boundaries and individual styles. [...] It is intended to account for types of electroacoustic music that are more concerned with varieties of

---

[6] The big difference between auditory and visual perception is that we can take in a sculpture as a whole the moment we see it, whereas the reception of a vocal music is temporal, which means we perceive it unfold over time and continually create possible meanings.

motion and flexible fluctuations rather than metrical time, more concerned with sounds whose sources and causes are relatively mysterious and ambiguous rather than blatantly obvious (Smalley 1997).

The concept of Smalley's *spectromorphology* is a tool for describing and analysing listening experiences. It refers to the interaction between sound spectra (spectro-) and the ways it changes and is shaped through time (-morphology). It offers a way of thinking which can be applied to a wide variety of (electroacoustic) music. As it concentrates on *intrinsic* features rather than on a range of possible contexts of the work, I apply his method of listening to vocal utterances. Nevertheless, music is a cultural construct, and an extrinsic foundation in culture is necessary so that the intrinsic can have meaning. The intrinsic and the extrinsic are interacting with each other.

2.1.2.1 From Extrinsic to Intrinsic Listening

How can vocalists induce reduced listening in the listener? How can we get from extrinsic to intrinsic listening? In vocal performance art, which treats almost all vocal utterances as musical events, a continuous trans-contextuality develops. The wide-open sound-world of individual vocal universes encourages imaginative and imagined extrinsic connections due to the variability and ambiguity of the given vocal material. On this subject, Pamela Z says:

> It seems like the difference between representational or figurative works and purely abstract work is almost like in visual art. Somebody is drawing or painting and is making a picture of someone or something or a situation versus making an image that is just a sort of layered form and abstract shapes that don't call to mind any specific object (Pamela Z 2021).

The listener's experience of listening to voices is a psychological process based on years of vocal communication. For example, when someone is crying out loudly, we may think of danger and not of a specific spectromorphological vocal sound. There is quite a difference between the following three statements, "someone lets out a cry", a second which says, "it sounds like someone crying", and a third which says, "it sounds as if behaving somebody crying" (Fig. 2.2).

In examples 2 and 3, we move from the purely extrinsic to more intrinsic qualities of specific musical listening. Here the focus is on acoustic microscopies of vocal sound-worlds, their flexible fluctuations, and their specific sounding aspects. Instead of referring to the source of the sound, we begin to listen to its sonic spectre and as composer–performers, we may sculpt the cry like a vocal phenomenon independent from any source.

The psychological attribution is not fixed but rather subject to revision. We may change our interpretation of the cry depending on the vocal sound that follows it. Equally, the psychological association might fade away if the cry is being repeated in a specific rhythmical grid, or if in an act of musical transition, the colour and dynamics change into bel canto singing as a result of a morphological process. Smalley defines it as: "The natural tendency to relate sounds to supposed sources and causes and to

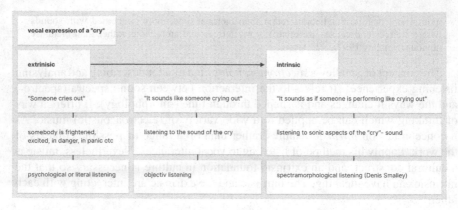

Fig. 2.2 From extrinsic to intrinsic threads, according to Smalley's spectromorphology. *Source* © Franziska Baumann

relate sounds to each other because they appear to have shared or associated origins." (Smalley 1997).

Suppose I, as a vocalist, reshape the cry into a cry-aria by concentrating on motivic developments of the produced cry. In that case, I am moving further away from the originally connoted expression. Similarly if I were to stretch the cry into a long-drawn-out high-pitched drone and to exclusively listen to timbres and fluctuations, that is, to the materiality of the sound. On the same subject, Pamela Z says:

> If you start a piece with breathing, a person might think about someone being out of breath, or being excited or tired. That's what the sound or action of breathing could represent, instead of thinking of the sound of breathing as something that sounds like white noise or a texture that gets a little thicker (Pamela Z 2021).

Or I may search for the limits of the scream material: extreme height and depth, dramatic volume, and limit of audibility. I am interested in the meaning-shift of physically produced vocal intensities and the particular aesthetics arising from this translation work. By shifting the focus of listening, vocal expressions are made perceptible less by their content than in their sonority. The tension between the extrinsic reference and the unfamiliar physicality is transferred to me as a performer through the internal production process. I increase my sensitivity to what subtle muscle adjustments lead to that sound and what small changes manifest in the sound and how this, in turn, can be perceived by the audience. Through the rehearsal process, the produced sonic pronouncements inscribe themselves in the body and thus become retrievable.

Through the renewed focus on vocal materiality, the meaning of a vocal expression changes gradually over the course of a piece. The improvised piece called *eaaa variations* (Minton 2015) by British avant-garde vocalist Phil Minton, is a perfect example of this. Using moaning and creaking sounds based on the vowels "eaaa", he explores and plays with coloration, pitch, duration, and the noise components of the vibrations. Even though he plays with musical variations of the same vowels and timbres, we as listeners permanently relate those sounds to extrinsic human meaning. Extrinsic perception which looks for content and character is inextricably linked to spectromorphological content, and most listeners find it difficult to put the focus on vocal phenomena as an independent experience. Minton plays with the listeners' expectation. When listening to his piece, we are made to constantly move back and forth between the extrinsic qualities of human utterance and the intrinsic spectral qualities that lead us towards a new aesthetic experience of vocal performance. When spectromorphology becomes the medium through which the voice can be explored and experienced, it becomes a new kind of "source" connection. Although Minton's musical composition is mostly abstract, he creates a strong image of *source bonding* (Smalley 1997) through gesture, mimicry and the nature of his physical presence. Smalley invented the term "source bonding" to represent this link between intrinsic and extrinsic threads. The vocal performer as a sound source on stage significantly influences how the meaning of vocal phenomena is transferred. The intentionally communicated varieties of gesture, facial expression and presence cannot be separated from the vocal sound event. Therefore, the performer has a substantial impact on how we perceive the utterances revealed through gesture and other physical activity in a stream of multilayered meaning (Fig. 2.3).

In his description of the listening process, Pierre Schaeffer (Schaeffer 1966)— whose work is mainly concerned with environmental and acoustic sounds—has identified four modes. The first mode is *information-gathering* which focuses on the message a sound carries. If I freely apply Schaeffer's first mode to our example of the cry, we are interested in who is crying and why. Maybe our neighbour is coming down the stairs screaming. We are wondering about possible motives behind the cry.

Schaeffer's second mode emphasises *passive reception*. We may hear somebody crying on the radio or far away in the street. While mode 1 focuses on the person of my attention, mode 2 concentrates on the subjective reaction to the sound of the cry. Modes 3 and 4 are concerned with listening for musical characteristics. Mode 4, *musical listening*, equates the listening to an explicitly musical language, whose meaning is unfolded by understanding its corresponding codes. Mode 3 represents

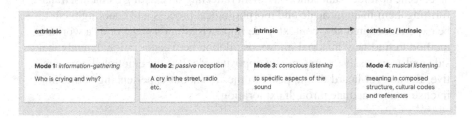

Fig. 2.3 From extrinsic to intrinsic threads, according to Schaeffer's listening modes. *Source* © Franziska Baumann

conscious listening to specific aspects of sound while disregarding any meaning that the sound might carry. This mode broadly coincides with Smalley's spectromorphological listening. Perception is focused on various spectromorphological aspects that are considered attractive, exciting or meaningful.

If we again refer to the example of the cry, a spectromorphological listening approach would in mode 3 examine it with regard to intrinsic aspects, pitch, type of attack, how it is sustained, changes of timbre and how it ends. Whereas in mode 4, we would have to look for a version in which the scream is set to music as an act of liberation, fear, or panic, be it experimental music theatre, hard rock, pop, opera or contemporary music.

I have freely extended Pierre Schaeffer's modes to the voice because it provides us with a differentiated way of focusing on extrinsic and intrinsic qualities. With regard to the cry, the contrast between modes 1 and 3 appears to be the most significant. Mode 1 points the listener to the extrinsic qualities outside the sound and to further possibilities of meaning, whereas mode 3 points to the intrinsic and abstract qualities of a sound.

None of the four modes is exclusive. The cry remains ambivalent, and most of the time, we interweave the different listening modes in a multidimensional network. Our attention switches between these levels and allows one level to be re-experienced through another. Since music happens on a timeline, perception changes over time. For example, vocal material with a specific emotional coloration, which is first heard as a figurative expression, undergoes a degree of abstraction through repetition.

Pamela Z describes this in her work:

> In my work, there is even a fight for dominance between representational or literal-like work that expresses an idea or a description of something versus work that is more abstract. I feel that part of me has always wanted to make very abstract work. But there's also another part that's easy to fall for. In works that are more literal or representational, that express something conceptually and are not just abstract, it's easier to find some handles to hold on to. So I always feel that there is a balance between these opposite poles (Pamela Z 2021).

Also my own music is not exclusively abstract and flirts with styles like bel canto, ethnic styles, jazz and also text. It is not my intention to look at traditional techniques and aesthetics through the eyes of serious music or to adopt them in an eclectic attitude. I am concerned with reflecting on existing elements, transforming them in an intricate and morphological process and enabling them to be experienced in a new context. Free improvisation on stage or as a working method to find new material allows oscillation between a rational, analytical side and an excessive, unrestrained opposite side. It is the emotional, imaginative, the not-yet-heard that appeals to me. It's about experiencing something intense and immediate through exploration.

2.1.2.2 Musicalising the Language

The wide-ranging utterances of the voice can also have a musical effect in language. When one leaves behind the semantic aspect of the voice, which links the words to intended meanings, one enters a space where the sound of the voice not only replaces the word (logos) but also enters into an "in-between" space, a vocal territory that unleashes a potential of multiperspectival impacts. When we move the focus from the semantic to the sonic level of a speech sound, the material aspect of the vocal expression comes to the fore. This notion of materiality contrasts with the idea of referentiality or semiotics. Materiality is about the sonic appearance and the effects associated with it. It emphasises the performative and musical dimensions of the voice that cannot be necessarily absorbed in a semantic-expressive function.

The question of the materiality of a linguistic event generates a shift of the listening focus from the "what" to the "how". Jenny Schrödl (2012) speaks of "the emotive dimension of vocal materiality instead of theatrical voices as a means of representing psychologically conceived characters" (translated by the author). This makes it possible to sketch a different and expanded idea of voices, or rather, vocal sound. If we listen to the musical materiality instead of the semantic content of speech, the attention switches to the interplay of parameters discussed above, such as pitch, dynamic, colour timbre, intonation, tempo and density. As a result, the linguistic utterance transforms from a meaning-bearing and expressive phenomenon to a musical phenomenon in its own right.

How can a composer or a performer overcome the unconscious intention to transmit words according to their semantic content? For instance, when developing my staged vocal performance *Liquid Souls* (Baumann 2011) for four singers, video and spatialised sound, I explored the vocal and gestural possibilities of the material disposition of speech fragments, statements and voice modules in collaboration with other vocalists. Since none of the singers had had any speech training, I instead emphasised the individual character of their voices. I asked them to use the immediacy of their bodily impulses in order to avoid the effort of creating any narrative meaning or correct pronunciation. Thus, I used bodily indications to focus attention on the production process itself and on the resulting materiality of the voice, which for example included the individual colouring of their voices. I had them run on stage shouting phrases simultaneously or reciting consonants, syllables, text fragments and vowels in choreographed sequences of lying, sitting and standing. I set microphones too high or too low so that they had to stretch and bend which has an effect on the vocal sound. As a result, shifts in the meaning of physically produced vocal intensities occurred, and a unique aesthetic emerged from this translation work. Words were made perceptible less in their content than in their sonority.

The tension between the textual content and the unfamiliar physicalities was transferred to the performers through the bodily production process. This, in turn, was perceptible to the audience. Throughout the rehearsal process, the linguistic utterances that were produced inscribed themselves in the body and thus became retrievable. The renunciation of the narrative as a unifying element is a decisive prerequisite to achieving vertical audibility.

What's interesting to note is that no voice doesn't mean anything. Every expression bears meaning information important to both yourself and those who perceive your performance. It doesn't matter if you present lyrics or if you make up your own gibberish kind of language that refuses linguistic semantics. What matters is to understand that the voice, per se, always brings along emotional information, which also is the case during vocal improvisations and inventions (Nowitz 2021).

By focusing on the "how" of the voice's appearance, we can detach speech from the semantic level, making phrases, words, syllables and sounds appear as sound phenomena, and offering them as hybrid musical material oscillating between meaning and sound.

The musicalisation of language opens up a *radical vocality* that far surpasses the idea of a musical landscape as a background or catalyst for one or more characters. It is the linguistic utterance which, in its pure sonority, itself becomes the vehicle for musical expression. In a process of permanent de- and re-contextualisation, the source of meaning-creation constantly changes between sound and language semantics. Although either the semantics of language or those of musicality may be foregrounded, the relationship between the two levels can be constantly renegotiated. Thus, a decentralised network of relations between the semantic and sonic levels of words and text emerges. Musical thinking allows for a more transparent sounding through (*Durchklingen*) because it liberates us from having to understand any particular content.

This focus of the material aspect of the spoken voice is part of new forms of postdramatic theatre, which Jenny Schrödl calls *Vocal Intensities* (Schrödl 2012). It refers to the voice as a musical–performative phenomenon and as a reality-creating force. Listening to a voice as an instrument and hearing its intrinsic qualities can be an extraordinarily creative process. To someone taking an interest in working with spectromorphological aspects, an infinite universe of sonic research opens up. The difficulty, however, can be how to put the extrinsic threads back in place as research is done at the lowest level of sound structure. Maintaining a realistic perceptual focus is a precarious balancing act.

2.1.3   Musicalising Radical Vocality with the Composer's Ear

When we leave aside the semantic, psychological and culturally connotated aspects of the voice, we move into a realm where the sound of the voice not only replaces word and meaning but enters an "in-between" space. This new area opens up the potential of multiperspective effects through *radical vocality*—a term coined by cultural theorist Pieter Verstraete. Radical vocality can be understood as a pervasive multiplicity of vocal art forms, orality, choral and vocal modalities, whose predominant objective is to recuperate the voice's distinct sounding and corporeal qualities from its signifying properties (Verstraete 2011).

Verstraete has defined radical vocality as a way of going against the grain of historical conventions and categories, which is reinforced by the combination of vocal performance art with digital audio technology. In the case of the disembodied or acousmatic voice, we experience the voice detached from the sound source. The vocal material sounds come to the listener from the loudspeakers without a human body and can be radically perceived in its materiality and vocal sonority through electronic modifications.

To me as a vocal performer–composer–improviser, radical vocality signifies an artistic technique that links inner imagination (authorship), simultaneous performance (interpretation), and auditory virtuosity (meaning-creation design). I present the voice as a sensual–material phenomenon in all its diversity. It unleashes power and sensual intelligence that enables the exploration of vocal characters, experimental vocal expressions and quick compositional thinking about shaping vocal parameters.

When I improvise, I use improvisational–compositional skills to shape my vocal intentions. Like a sculptor, I ask myself: How do I shape my vocal material? Like a musical dramaturg, I focus on the question: How do I relate my vocalisation to what has been and to what will be? Like a musical director, I interrogate the internal relationship of the sounds to each other: How do I modulate the sounds' functions of accompanying, supporting, contrasting, etc.? How do I place my vocal sounds in the context of other digital or analogue sound sources, vocalists, or instrumentalists? And like a listening virtuoso, I may question my focus of attention: Which aspects of vocal spectromorphologies do I listen to in the different moments?

With an ear trained on intrinsic qualities, I have a multitude of decision-making options available at any given point. The power of decision that manifests itself from moment to moment shapes the internal structure and, ultimately, the form of the piece. The spectromorphological approach is a necessary aid to any compositional process. Simultaneously retaining an alert perceptual focus on the intrinsic and extrinsic threads, which means constantly being aware of and integrating what the audience might be perceiving, constitutes a precarious balancing act in a constant multi-perspective game.

In this chapter, attention has been drawn to abstract listening with a spectromorphological ear where the vocal artist's perception as a composer–performer–improviser can be different from that of other listeners. It is an investigative process in which spectromorphological details and inherent aspects of the material itself are explored. It implies the detachment of the vocal sound from the sound source. In this process, the instrumental–extrinsic threads are blocked in order to concentrate on refining spectromorphological details and sound qualities. This kind of listening is thus an abstract, relatively objectified process, a microscopic, intrinsic listening.

The creative potentials of spectromorphological and reduced listening is what I mean by musicalising the radical vocality. This helps us understand the mediated voice as an abstract vocal terrain, the topic which I will explore in the next chapter.

References

Ihde D (2007) Listening and voice: phenomenologies of sound, 2nd edn. State University of New York Press, Albany, NY

Kohl MA (2015) Vokale Performancekunst als feministische Praxis. Bielefeld: transcript Verlag

La Barbara J (1976) Interviewed by Walter Zimmermann in Desert plants: conversations with 23 American musicians. Vancouver, Walter Zimmermann and A.R.C. Publications. http://beginner-press.de/wp-content/uploads/2017/08/desert_plants_web.pdf. Accessed 9 Aug 2022

Monk M (1997) Notes on the voice. In: Jowitt D (ed) Meredith Monk. Baltimore, John Hopkins University Press

Nattiez J-J (1990) Music and discourse: towards a semiology of music. Princeton University Press, Princeton

Nowitz A (2019) Doctoral thesis, Stockholm University of the Arts, University College of Opera. Monsters I Love: On Multivocal Arts. http://uniarts.diva-portal.org/smash/record.jsf?pid=diva2%3A1283884&dswid=-5597. Accessed 9 Aug 2022

Oehlschlägel R (1984) Female structuralist performancemaker: versuch über Laurie Anderson. In: Henck H, Gronemeyer G, Richards D (eds), Neuland, Ansätze zur Gegenwart 4, 254–258

Piana G (1998) Philosophy of music and its aim. A brief account. Axiomathes 9:213–22. https://doi.org/10.1007/BF02681713. Accessed 9 Aug 2022

Schaeffer P (1966) Traité des objects musicaux. Revised 1977. Paris: Edition du Seuil

Schrödl (2012) Vokale Intensitäten: Zur Ästhetik der Stimme im postdramatischen Theater. Bielefeld, Transkript Verlag

Smalley D (1997) Spectromorphology: explaining sound-shapes. Organised Sound 2(2):107–126. https://doi.org/10.1017/S1355771897009059. Accessed 9 Aug 2022

Verstraete P (2011) Vocal extensions, disembodied voices in contemporary music theatre and performance. https://www.academia.edu/3035586/Vocal_Extensions_Disembodied_Voices_in_Contemporary_Music_Theatre_and_Performance. Accessed 8 Aug 2022

Weber-Lucks T (2008) Doctoral thesis, Technische Universität Berlin, Fakultät Geisteswissenschaften. Vokale Performancekunst als neue musikalische Gattung. https://depositonce.tu-berlin.de/handle/11303/2308. Accessed 9 Aug 2022

Listening examples

Baumann F (2011) Liquid souls. http://baumann-brieske.net/projects/liquid-souls/. Accessed 9 Aug 2022

Minton P (2015) eaaa variations. https://www.youtube.com/watch?v=Dp3K_MX7ANQ. Accessed 9 Aug 2022

Full interviews

Nowitz A (2021) Interview. http://www.franziskabaumann.ch/en/press/interview2-nowitz.php. Accessed 12 Aug 2022

Pamela Z (2021) Interview. http://www.franziskabaumann.ch/en/press/interview1-pamela.php. Accessed Aug 2022

Chapter 3
The Mediated Voice

Abstract This chapter aims to introduce perspectives for understanding the mediated and then disembodied voice in human–computer interaction. My argument starts with two basic notions. First, I introduce the mediated voice as an *electrified space of vocal expression*. As voices "from me" or as "clones of myself", they are modified through electrified processes and become reflections and distortions of the original voice. Secondly, the mediated voice is explored in prerecorded vocal elements and spatialised disembodied vocal clips as "myths of disembodied voices" that can animate a body in our imagination. Next, I discuss four vocal domains that contribute to meaning in vocal music in human–computer interaction. To do this, I will introduce a brief theoretical framework for understanding *persona references* in the mediated voice. These illustrate vocal phenomena associated with identities such as articulation, affect, physicality and language. The persona references each describe a significant area of the voice in electroacoustic music and thus the mediated voice. Through analysing some examples, this chapter will illuminate the nature of the mediated voice using insight from listening examples and practice-based research.

3.1 Introduction

Up to this point in our discussion, the embodied voice could be characterised as monophonic. But through technology it finds response through speakers and electronic modifications; it becomes an "echo" that takes up the languages of imaginative processes: vocalising, playing and listening become polyphonic. As a vocalist, I not only hear my embodied voice, I *listen to* myself outside or from myself.

The important difference between the embodied voice and the voice mediated by a gestural interface lies in the physicality and the non-corporeality. In the embodied voice, the body is the interface, and in the mediated voice, we listen to the vocal sounds without a body (because decoupling from the body has taken place). It is not a vibrating instrument like a clarinet but a digitised representation of the body's vibrations. The vocal sound comes to the listener from the loudspeakers without a human body and can be radically perceived in its materiality and vocal sonority

F. Baumann, *Embodied Human—Computer Interaction in Vocal Music Performance*, SpringerBriefs in Cultural Computing, https://doi.org/10.1007/978-3-031-17985-3_3

through electronic modifications. We can point to the original embodied voice and its personality by employing gestural systems. In that sense, we can consider the mediated or disembodied voice as an echo we touch again. Furthermore, the mediated voice can evoke imaginary bodies in our imagination as we try to understand whose voice is mediated.

With its electronic technology, the machine is used to access, generate, explore and configure vocal sound materials, a process in which loudspeakers are the prime medium of transmission. Already the types of microphone and amplifier are modifiers of this transmission. They determine the electrical space in which the voice operates. Sonic elements at the lower threshold of hearing can easily reach the ears of the listeners, individual frequencies can be improved with more energy, and a vocal soundscape can be created.

Sound recording makes it possible to compose directly with the vocal sound and allows immediate and sensual access to vocal parameters. It facilitates the composition of a sustained project with musical and vocal parameters that are difficult to notate, such as particular multivocal techniques and subtle tonal, rhythmic and tonal inflections.

The amplification and modification of the voice also influence body awareness and felt sense. If, as a singer, I play with an amplified voice, the extremity of my body sound is expanded, which results in feedback to my kinesthetic sensation—I experience my body as more extensive in an amplified environment. In contrast, the kinesthetic experience in an anechoic and dry space is entirely different. There, my body perception is shrinking. I perceive my body dimensions as small compared to the surrounding space. Using the machine, I expand and shrink my body through electronic distance and achieve—at least theoretically—objectification of my female body and voice. It allows the electrified and disembodied voices to be enveloped in new imaginative bodies.

I invite the reader to imagine the mediatisation of the voice in two ways:

- First, as an *electrified space of vocal expression*. As voices "from me" or as "clones of myself", they are modified through electrified processes and become reflections and distortions of the original voice.
- Secondly, I explore the mediated voice as prerecorded vocal elements and spatialised disembodied vocal clips as "myths of bodyless voices" that can animate a body in our imagination.

I discuss the imaginative mode's extended modality of ongoing experience. This mode identifies how the digitalisation of the embodied voice stimulates imaginary bodies through its presence and construction and pinpoints the meaning these create within music-making. It is not a matter of observation of technical novelty or an opinion of feeling for an acousmatic piece but rather an evaluation of how the presence of the electronically modified disembodied and spatialised voice shifts the way we relate to, interpret or perceive it.

To orientate ourselves within the shifting nature of these relationships between the embodied and the mediated voice, I present four vocal domains contributing or co-creating within the human–computer interaction. Therefore, I will introduce a short theoretical framework for understanding the *persona references* in the disembodied voice. These elucidate vocal phenomena associated with intrinsic identities. Each domain of experience illustrates a significant area of the acousmatic and thus of the mediated voice. By analysing a few examples, the chapter highlights the nature of the mediated voice using insights gained from listening examples and practice-based research. I will evaluate the shifting nature of these domains as they conduct, co-operate and collaborate within the flow of time and music-making.

3.1.1 The Electrified Space of Vocal Expression

The electrified space of vocal expression draws attention to the sonic developments fed directly from the vocal source. It encompasses all aspects of the experience of acousmatic and electroacoustic vocality that are heard indirectly as a product of the vocal performer but are related to causes outside the body. Specifically, this is focusing on those aspects that can be attributed to electronic manipulations that provide a direct kind of control or influence on sound modification and the effects on sound distribution in space. As an immediate reflection, extension, and distortion of the live voice, the electrified space encompasses a listening environment of the disembodied vocal sound that still has the properties of the vocal input.

The sonic exploration of the voice using digital processing opens up abundant vocal sound fields that otherwise remain hidden. For vocalists, doors open into the virtual, unimaginable worlds of vocal sound, which in turn can influence their vocal practice as singers. For me, this made processes audible, which inspired my compositional practice as a vocalist in the sense that I tried to imitate what I heard from electronic manipulation (Fig. 3.1).

For Pamela Z, the most significant influence on finding her voice as an artist was when she started using electronics and playing with processing her voice with digital delay and reverb. On this she said:

> When I started doing that, I began to completely start listening differently and organising sound and music in a new way. I became interested in repetition and pattern, which significantly impacted how I composed music and listened (Pamela Z 2021).

Once amplified, processed and explored, the richness of vocal sounds is exposed for detailed listening. We can immerse ourselves in the smallest vocal sound moments, compose them further in layers, and still these small grains remain spectacularly intimate. Or, as Donna Hewitt says:

> Electroacoustic technologies allow us to overcome certain biological, physical, and emotional limitations of natural embodied voice (Hewitt 2006).

The alternation between embodied voice and voice manipulated by the machine occurs at various opposite poles: corporeality versus incorporeality, closeness versus distance, one voice and many voices, clarity and distortion, real body and imaginative body (Fig. 3.2).

Fig. 3.1 Pamela Z in her studio in San Francisco. *Source* © Goran Vejvoda

Fig. 3.2 Franziska Baumann performing at ICLI, International Conference on Live Interfaces, Trondheim 2020. *Source@* Shreejay Shrestha

Re-Shuffling Sirenes

In this piece, I couple the electronic modifications very close to my voice, creating a convolutionary extension into Ambisonic[1] spatialisation, thus extending my body without creating independent clones. The intermittent standing feedback of my voice is transformed into a distortion so that it is no longer heard as a clone but only as a spatialised noise. The human–machine interaction expands my body together with "From Me" out there (Baumann 2020).

Switching between the embodied and mediated voice creates a hybrid in the body awareness and the felt sense, not only for me as a performer but also for the audience. Members of the audience tell me that it is weird to perceive my body as usual again after a concert. The human–machine interaction on stage leads to an enlargement of my body, my aura, and they have to dispel this enlargement when they talk to me after the performance. I create enlarged vocal identities of myself, and my body connects to them with gestural communication.

See Fig. 3.3.

Kristin Norderval calls the mediated voice "From Me but Not Me". She describes this as:

> With the Embodied Voice, I know exactly what I can do and how I can control it. With the Mediated Voice, my composer brain decides what to do with the "From Me". I can control and shape it directly within the structure of a framework of chosen tools. It becomes a collaborator in the unpredictability and possible randomness of how this mediated voice overlaps in time with my embodied live voice (Norderval 2021).

The manipulated voice can thus be experienced as an extension of the body or as a collaborator depending on the unpredictability of the sonic processes.

Alex Nowitz sees the central aspect of the mediated voice as creating a kind of "new" voice through playing with live electronics and merging the live voice with the sampled clone:

> When you create vocal copies of yourself, you create a tiny fragment of your soul. This spiritual aspect is embedded in this practice [...] I still consider the "Clones of Myself" to be part of me because I still change and manipulate them by changing the pitch, making a glissando out of it so on. There are tons of ways to manipulate the clones through different applications (Nowitz 2021).

Fig. 3.3 Zoom Interview in 2021: Kristin Norderval in Oslo and Franziska Baumann in Berne. *Source* © Franziska Baumann

---

[1] See note 23.

Pamela Z considers the entire apparatus of her voice and the processing of it as her instrument:

> When I am singing and processing my voice in real-time, it is very organic to me. It is not like something that I feel is artificial. And also, it does not feel like it is external or outside of me. It feels like it is all one unified part of what I am doing. Often when I compose works for my voice and electronics, I do not just start by just singing and then saying: now what processing can I add to this? It happens simultaneously. I turn everything on, and my voice immediately goes into the MAX patch. Then I have set up that patch to apply various types of processing like delays, loops, granulation, reverberation, or pitch shifting. But all of that is happening in real-time (Pamela Z 2021).

As for the technical side, the electrified space of vocal expression includes any device that in any way affects or modifies the vocal sound. Exploring electronic processes such as shuffling, feedback, loops, granulation, delays, reverb, pitch-shifting and others allow us singers to break out of our habits and find new forms of vocal expression. I perceive the so-called effects not simply as effects because they offer compositional tools similar to composing for choirs, for example. They can refer to imaginative processes and also to conditions that take place in reality. Granulation, for example, could be perceived as a process of disintegration and dissolution of identity, reverberation as expansion into infinity, delay as the echo of an echo, feedback as a rising distorted wall and the superimpositions of one's own voice as schizophrenic multiplications. The fuzzy edges of electronic vocal modulations allow me to explore a fantastic realm of disembodied vocal terrain that I can shape and interact with using gestural systems (Fig. 3.4).

Pamela Z never refers to sonic manipulations as effects because they are part of her music:

> They are layers of music. It would be the same when somebody writes a piece of choral music where the soprano is the music, and all the other three voices are just effects being put on that (laughing) (Pamela Z 2021).

Alex Nowitz sees the direct influence on sound modification as a way to create a mixture of acoustic voice and live electronics and to compose complex vocal textures:

Fig. 3.4 Zoom Interview in July 2021: Pamela Z in San Francisco and Franziska Baumann in Crete. *Source* © Franziska Baumann

It's like putting up multiple mirrors around me that I am *looking at*, which is fascinating and weird at the same time [...] The clone or *Doppelgänger* is dissolving into its live voice, and the live voice is dissolving into its *Doppelgänger* (Nowitz 2021).

I consider the acoustic clones of my voice as parts of my original voice simply because I still use them during the performance and manipulate them by changing pitches and sound frequencies, creating glissandi, and so on. The difference with the live voice is that the electroacoustic clones can now be controlled or imaginatively touched by my hands and arms. The way I play gesturally with the vocal clones then changes the perception of the musical material.

These "in-between" worlds make me listen. They expand my compositional ideas and lift the mundane out of the ordinary. Maintaining this primal relationship to the human while generating new vocal phenomena with the computer are exciting artistic processes. New imaginary vocal worlds can emerge that let us imagine natural choirs and vocal multiplications, sometimes reflecting traditional ideas of counterpoint and multivocality but opening up into fascinating new listening spaces.

3.1.2 Co-presence of the Imaginative

In view of the plethora of never-before-heard sounds and noises, the voice inevitably forms a counterweight to the disembodiment through technology—and thus to the physical experience of the audience. One could say that these disembodied voices place a "phantasmagorical" veil over the sensory apparatus (Ihde 2007). In interactive human–computer interaction, this veil is further extended by a sense of the mystical surrounding technology and an acousmatisation of the voice. The voice belongs to a vaster polyphony of perceptual and imaginative experience (Ihde 2007).

Following Pierre Schaefer's reduced listening and Denis Smalley's spectromorphological listening, I relate the electrified space of vocal expression in its acousmatic appearance to the co-presence of the imaginary. The imaginative mode opens up what Godøy calls the epistemology of simulations (Godøy 1997). By this, he means the possibility of creating variants of sound objects in which one particular feature or aspect is changed while others remain the same, and then observing and comparing the effects of these changes on the experience.

If I record my voice, it becomes an event detached from my body. With electronic manipulations, the differences in sonic properties can evoke other body imaginings. For example, loops or delays can simulate an augmentation of my person. However, when I heavily granulate my live voice and add feedback, I create such a strong abstraction that the voices become alienated from my body and simulate entities in their own right.

Ihde describes imagination as an "excess" that carries it beyond perception. Hidden in this "excess" are both certain aspects of "self-presence" and a fundamental liaison with the world. The "innermost" is not distant from the "outermost" (Ihde 2007). For example, I hear a friend's voice. I close my eyes, and now I can remember the sound of her voice. I can even read a text and apply her vocal sound-print to words she has not said before. The never-before spoken words contain variations of her "self-presence". The inwardly heard representations of vocal and sonic events can take various forms, such as memories, flashbacks, fantasies, etc., but in any case they show themselves unreal. The imaginary presence of the inner voice that belongs to her remains hidden from the other.

The imaginative mode in the electrified space of vocal expression contains variations of "self-presence" within itself. These electronically processed voices can decouple from the monophonic vocal source as independent vocal phenomena. Just as I can wilfully and imaginatively associate my friend's voice with new words, the mediated voice may initiate variations of body references.

3.1.2.1 Myths of Disembodied Vocal Terrain

From myths, we know disembodied voices such as Sybille, the Sphinx, the Sirens, Narcissus and Echo (Weigel 2006). For example, in the legend of Sybille, the voice appears as the remnant of a human figure that has survived the physical decay, the dissolution of the body, and has thus overcome mortality.[2]

Something similar happens to the nymph Echo, in whose case the dwindling body is not the effect of decay, however, but of lovesickness, whereby the fact that she distorts herself in love is already attributed as an effect of her distorted voice. Echo can only reproduce what she hears and therefore suffers from the impossibility of confessing her love to her beloved Narcissus. He, whose words are repeated by his beloved Echo in a mutilated form, feels betrayed by the nymph and therefore rejects her. She hides in the woods, and her miserable body hungers for him. Only her voice and bones remain. While her bones become stones, her voice endures.

For us, Ovid's story of these remaining voices can be read as an art myth, representing an initial artistic set-up, as a primary dimension of the mediated voice that detaches from the body and manifests in disembodied sound. If the modified voices decouple and become separated, independent clones of the singer emerge. We find ourselves in a vocal arena of alienation on the one hand and the emergence of new identities on the other.

In this sense, the imaginative mode opens up disembodied vocal insights with an illusion of vocal presence. In the seemingly insubstantial flow of events, we may experience changing identities of the embodied voice.

---

[2] Ovid, Metamorphosis: "usque adeo mutata ferar, nullique videnda,/ voce tamen noscar, vocem mihi fata relinquent" (XIV, 152f). "I will be so changed and now and nowhere to be seen, / but I will be recognised by the voice, fate will leave me a voice." (translated by the author).

3.1.2.2 Physical-Emotional Access to the Imaginary

Just as ambivalent as the digital achievements for society can be considered, my work is also not designed to make a clear, unambiguous statement. They should instead offer vocal worlds and make them physically-emotionally experienceable. There is always a clear commitment to the sensual in music—to all that can only be experienced by hearing and performing. The ambivalence is to be made into a confrontation with the world of vocal sound, respectively, the multivocal voice of the embodied and disembodied voice.

That's why very different feedback comes back concerning the disembodied voices. For example, listeners may be concerned with gender issues and hear various gender aspects in the vocal expressions. As Marit van-de-Haar, in her Master Thesis, wrote about one of my solo performances:

> By making excessive use of her voice, combining it with technology, she creates distance from the objectification of both her female body and her voice and she—at least theoretically—disrupts any attempt of the seduction-related signification of her body and voice. Aside from that, she explicitly makes the audience aware of the different uses of the male and the female voice within opera by portraying both roles herself (Van-de-Haar 2020).

My dual identity as a composer–performer places me often in between two activities, as Hanna Bosma argues in relation to electroacoustic music:

> The composer-vocalists take both the masculine position of the composer (determining structure) and the feminine position as a vocalist (producing vocal sound) (Bosma 2013).

Moreover, I want to offer an experience in which the vocal phenomena manipulated in the computer trigger an auditory sensibility that transcends the boundaries of traditional roles towards the imaginary. (Fig. 3.5)

I like to start a piece with a vocal sound idea rooted in my body's felt sense. For example, I begin with an articulatory expression that connects with a specific gestural idea for the resulting disembodied voice. Through practice, I feel an imaginary kinaesthetic touch for the disembodied vocal idea. The imagined *touch* as a way to communicate vocal sounds is an intrinsic part of my approach to gestural sensory technology. There might be an idea of what kind of feeling is associated with the interlinked gestural concept of the embodied and disembodied voice, whether it needs language, words, or just vocal sound. Research on a particular topic, such as glacial movement (Fig. 3.5), can offer an artistic perspective to my vocal and gestural approaches. Exploration in the studio includes physical experimentation with sensors and related sound processes, refining movement vocabularies, assembling compositional ideas, and calibrating responsiveness and dialogue with the system.

As it goes on, composing is more of an intuitive thing, a more profound listening to what the piece wants and finding a balance between the elements of the machine's restrictions and the idea of touch and vocal imaginary. I remind

Fig. 3.5 Franziska Baumann on the Rhone Glacier, Switzerland, 2003. *Source* © Daniel Repond

myself to be playful, ask questions, and initiate discoveries. It's about keeping the focus and, at the same time, being completely open, being vulnerable rather than showing. It is about the poetry of the senses that interrupts allocentric listening. There are phases of an unrestrained ecstatic way of working, in which I translate—with a heightened sensitivity—everything I perceive into a specific work. These can also be visual impulses. Inspired by the principle of "automatic writing", intuitively drawn sound graphics can generate impulses for disembodied and spatially moving vocal landscapes (Fig. 3.5).

When I compose with recorded vocal sounds, I walk the line between sensory perception and the physical experience of the audience. How far do

I move away from the original voice, and to what extent do I let it swell into multiplied voices that take on new identities? (Fig. 3.6)

Fig. 3.6 Franziska Baumann Drawing—Imaginary Music. *Source* © Franziska Baumann

3.1.3 Vocal Identities and Persona References

After introducing the electrified space of vocal expression and the mediated voice, in which I discussed the co-presence of the imaginative mode, I would like to elaborate on some features associated with the voice and its representation of identity. In doing so, I aim to unravel some of the multidimensional elements in the hybrid realm of the voice in human–computer interaction, to allow us to better understand the relationship of voice, identity and body.

When listening to imaginative voices and bodies, variants of persona references can emerge. The *persona references* in the mediated or acousmatic voice emphasise the imaginative in the mediated voice. Extra-musical aspects such as identity, language, physicality and emotionality create different levels of meaning within the musical process. As mentioned above, the voice is not just a source sound like any other. The voice has a special status for humans across cultures. It is the original verbal and non-verbal communication vehicle and one of the most primal "instruments" of musical expression. We primarily want to understand the message of vocal utterances because we are all carriers of an individual voice.

As we have seen in the discussion of spectromorphological listening, this is reflected in perceptual sensitivity to vocal sounds, to the meaning that these sounds can convey, be they linguistic, identity-related or affective. This sensitivity occurs at a very early stage of our human development. We first listen to voices before we can speak. It is of existential importance to our existence to understand and interpret the voice of those closest to us.

As Smalley's spectromorphological listening reveals, the flow and length of events fundamentally impact the associated perception between extrinsic and intrinsic threads. When a cry is stretched and multiplied, we experience perceptual variations, from gathering information, to consciously listening to sonic aspects of the cry, or subsequently to an event that implies new vocal agency and thus imaginative "persona" specifications.

For Smalley, the occurrence of the voice in an electroacoustic piece will entail a perceptual shift when introduced:

> The moment a voice is perceived in a sounding context, the listener's ear is drawn to it, and interpretation shifts focus on the unseen human presence, trying to decode the meaning of its utterances and the relationship between the person to the sounding environment [...] a human presence where there previously was none changes everything (Smalley 1996).

As a singer playing with sensor live technology, I find myself in a hybrid field of acoustic signs referencing persons and imaginative reconfigurations. I expose multilayered points of persona references and transcend the boundaries of the relationship to the body, gender, age, emotions and feelings through the mediated voice and its electronic modifications. As the word *persona* suggests, the voice is a sounding through. If I change some parameters, the mediated voice describes a different persona—it morphs into an alienated clone of myself. For example, if I change the speed of my mediated voice, the energy components in the formants change, and the expression of my voice becomes detached from my person.

Depending on the electronic modification, the corporeality of the digitalised voices can morph into a pure acousmatic sound which no longer has any reference to the human. A high level of abstraction can easily cross the boundary of the concrete voice so that one no longer recognises the original voice as a sound source and the persona disappears. For example, if I create a standing, distorted vocal feedback, a noisy wall appears to which one no longer attributes a human entity.

Given this imaginative presence of the mediated voice and a presumption about what is happening at a particular perceptual level, the question of structural features becomes one of the more subtle and careful variations in the imaginative threshold.

To illuminate the referential boundaries of *persona* in the mediated voice, I will adopt a taxonomy described by Andreas Bergsland (2010). He proposes four experiential domains to understand listening experiences in electroacoustic vocal music and to find appropriate terms to describe different vocal aspects. The four domains distinguish persona references of body, identity, affect and language. This model, illustrated with concrete examples and quotes from my interviewees, offers perspectives on mediated voice in human–computer interaction that match human references within the live electronically altered and the acousmatic voice.

The framework incorporates philosophies and theories from a transdisciplinary perspective and integrates ideas about the relationship to the phenomenology of listening to voices (Ihde 2007), experiencing voices in electroacoustic music (Bergsland 2010), aesthetics of the voice in postdramatic theatre (Schrödl 2012), body, media, music, body discourses in music after 1950 (Drees 2011) and the unmasking of the disembodied voice (Verstraete 2011).

3.1.3.1 The Articulation Domain

The articulation domain identifies the physical perception of the voice to ascertain the primary sensory input as the basis of body information. It involves all physiological organs and the movement and behaviour during vocalisation, which we perceive primarily in vocal *articulation*. The articulation domain addresses different levels of auditory imagination and the extent to which we listen to mediated voices that trigger other "body" references. Do I listen to a sound of a body, or do I listen to a sound without a body?

Articulation refers to "how" the vocal sound is produced and how the vocal apparatus is set in motion. It relates to articulatory aspects related to how vocal sounds are produced. We link directly to the physical source of the voice. We listen to the vocal apparatus and the individual vocal sound. We hear how the vocal folds start to move, what tension the surrounding muscles create, and whether the voice sounds free, pressed, breathy, rough, soft or metallic. We hear how lips, tongue, jaw and glottis produce sounds and noises. We hear the body materiality in sounding action.

For example, we can hear and kinesthetically track how someone breathes, rhythmically transitioning the inhale and exhale into a groove and thereby causing the diaphragm to move into action. We may listen to how someone slowly begins to whisper and increasingly vibrates the vocal folds, clearly expanding the sound into the resonant chambers of the nasal area and condensing it into a scream. We may feel the subglottic pressure when a vocalist produces a multiphonic sound. We may feel pressure in our glottis as our mirror neurons provide us with a kinaesthetic stimulus.

Stops and clicks, and plosives like [p], [t] and [k] are exponents of articulatory behaviour. Fricatives like [s] and [f] have a characteristic sound spectrum with significant energy in the high-frequency range. Oscillators like the French uvular [r] or the rolling [r] in Spanish and various Swiss and other dialects produce periodic oscillations. The position of lips, tongue and mouth are usually associated with speech production. That is why we call them articulatory factors, with which an incredible variety of sounds can be produced.

Singers and vocalists can accurately analyse how sound production feels kinaesthetic. There is a reason why singers with an acute voice problem are forbidden not only to sing, but also to listen to vocal music—because the body automatically puts itself into a vocalising position when listening.

Within the articulation domain, we may analyse how phonation would feel under these imaginary conditions. We could consider it as the maximal voice if we are able to imagine ourselves producing similar sounds or if the mediated voices transport an image of a body. It may be reflected in how we describe vocal sounds: it sounds tense or relaxed because we know how it would feel to make it. But, for example, if we tune the sampled voice significantly down, we don't know what it would feel like to reproduce that vocal sound: that mediated voice triggers an imaginary body, probably a vast body. With the artificially pitched-down voice, we could realise a minimal voice because it is a non-imaginable body.

Paul Lansky, *Idle Chatter*, 1985.

An example of the articulation domain in electronic music is Paul Lansky's *Idle Chatter* (Lansky 1985). The piece was made using a process called linear predictive coding, an analysis tool that essentially breaks down the digitally recorded human voice into sibilants, plosives, and the remaining buzz of the vocal cords, and granular synthesis, where sounds are broken down into small "grains" and then transposed and layered. The articulation and the pitch of the artificial voices let us imagine women's bodies. The metallic overtone could also refer to pubescent boys. The not quite clear "persona" with rather minimal identity references in articulations make us listen and evoke our imagination.

Joachim Heintz, *Alma*, 2018.

In *Alma*, we hear a woman's voice and its live electronic modifications, which come very close to the original voice and appear as echoes (Heintz 2018). They occasionally manifest themselves multiplied and then disappear again. Since the reference to the vocal source is always present, we can perceive them as commentators, as manifold, re-acting clones of the original voice, since they always remain powerfully articulated.

Alex Nowitz, *Panache*, 2019.

In *Panache*, Alex Nowitz is articulating mouth sounds without sound, we hear his tongue and lips in action (Nowitz 2019).

3.1.3.2 The Identity Domain

The identity domain defines how voices evoke meaning through their presence and construction of gender, age, personhood and social aspects. These aspects can convey themselves through specific types of sound such as tinny, breathy, rough, bright, etc. Our ears unconsciously want to perceive the meaning and the message of the persona (Ihde 2007). Who is on stage? The voice always enters into a relationship of personal mediation, and it moves, touches, captivates, repels or disgusts. Voices are unique. No two voices sound the same. Even if they have undergone years of classical training, we recognise the interpreter. We have preferences for singers' voices, some lift us into enchanted spheres, aim at our heart, evoke undreamt of feelings, take us away from everyday life, and others repel us.

The experiential domain of identity can be regarded as the "Who"–domain since it deals with recognition, identification, categorisation of the identity of the vocal persona of the listener (Bergsland 2010).

Categories such as gender, age, personality, ethnicity, size, regional accent and dialect can potentially be recognised from the voice, depending on the availability of cues and the experience and background of the listener. The wide field of interaction with the mediated voice makes it possible to play with different attributes of identity (Fig. 3.7).

Kristin Norderval, *Flying Blind*, 2021

In Flying Blind, singer and composer Kristin Norderval creates several clones of her voice (Norderval 2021). The electronic counterparts are unchanging in their acoustic appearance and oscillate as choral diversifications. Although the embodied voice is multiplied by three delay buffers, the identity of the clones remains constant in the spatialised arrangement.

Fig. 3.7 Kristin Norderval performing *Flying Blind*, 2021. *Source* © Petra Dollemann

Franziska Baumann, *Hunting Tectonics*, 2020.

I sing an f" (an octave above middle F) and switch from this high register directly to subharmonic singing by making other parts of the larynx sound like the pocket folds (Baumann 2020). The first subharmonic is sung to appear an octave below the low singing voice and recorded with a contact microphone that I directly put on my throat. Overlapping loops and their spatialisation lead to a distortion that may be reminiscent of—rather male—primordial beings and counterpoint the high female vocal passages.

Pamela Z, *Span*, 2017.

Pamela Z manipulates her voice through fragmentation and delay (Pamela Z 2017). The pitch remains the same, but the cut-up fragments of her acoustic fingerprint offer new insights into possible new, smaller identities. She says that a big difference is the type of processing she uses in her compositions. For example, on using delay she says:

> It allows me to do things that, without it, I would need a choir or an ensemble to perform the same things because I am creating a sound, then I am bringing back, and I am building new sounds on top of that layer (Pamela Z 2021).

Despite the multiplication of voices, the identity references remain identical (Fig. 3.8).

Alex Nowitz, *Mundfundstücke*, 2017.

In the first part of his piece *Mundfundstücke* for voice and Strophonion, Nowitz sings long tones with a slight colouring (Nowitz 2017). His electronically generated "vocal ghosts" experience pitch and formant changes, and we can identify many of the same but also imaginary other male voices around him. The sudden rise in pitch may suggest female sirens.

Electronic manipulations can contribute to projecting different kinds of identities. These identities can even gradually change or be superimposed on a type of metamorphosis of transformation.

3.1.3.3 The Affect Domain

The affect domain defines the emotion-specific patterns that convey meaning through their colour and pinpoints the affectual connections they create within the vocal sound. It embraces a range of phenomena, including attitudes, interpersonal dialogues, moods, emotions. All these phenomena are in principle encountered in electroacoustic music. As I discussed in Chap. 1, spectromorphological or reduced listening may change our listening focus from extrinsic to intrinsic aspects of the vocal sound. With an experimental approach to vocalising, a formerly emotional expression may become pure sound. Vice versa, by applying different types of affective

Fig. 3.8 Alex Nowitz performing the Strophonion. *Source* © Joachim Liebe

colouring into phonemes, syllables, words, phrases, and the *empty voice*,[3] the sonic material is communicated in emotion-specific patterns. Vocalisations that are powerfully charged with emotions do sometimes appear in contemporary music such as Ligeti's *Aventures* (1962), Berio's *Sequenza III* (1965), Aperghis' *Récitations* (1978), Cathy Berberian's *Stripsody* (1976), or in electroacoustic music such as Berio's *Visage* (1961, on Berio & Maderna, 2006). In *Red Bird*, Trevor Wishart directed the vocalists to apply different types of affective colouring to several phonemes, syllables, words and phrases in order to project such implications into phonemic objects themselves (Wishart, 1996).

In *Telefon Arie*, a piece I performed as part of *Gravity Pleasures* in the snow on the Swisscom Tower in Berne (Fig. 3.9), I apply various affects to fragments that appear dissociative and fragmentary, interrupted by gesturally triggered sounds. The piece is about artificial emotions in telephone queues and answering machines that suggest intimacy without a person being present. The type of writing and the colours in Fig. 3.10 indicate a specific affect such as fast and stuttering, spoken restlessly with a high voice, rushed, consonants, explosive spite, wild screeching, laughing, mocking or very happy, ecstatic and coloratura, fast and pointillistic, etc.

---

[3] By the "empty voice" I mean for example vocal expressions of relief, groan, shock, etc. without words or syllables.

Fig. 3.9 Franziska Baumann performing *Telefon Arie* at *Gravity Pleasures* on the Swisscom Tower Berne 2018. *Source* © Ane Hebeisen

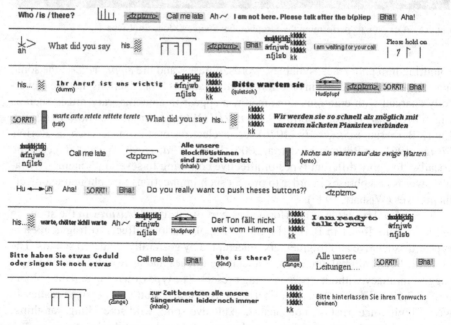

Fig. 3.10 *Telefon Arie*, piece for solo voice and live electronics. *Source* © Franziska Baumann

Live electronic modifications can alter the cues on which emotional decoding depends. They can change or even emphasise the emotional content. Studies show that a large part of the information is conveyed emotionally. Listeners across cultures and languages can recognise emotions from content-free speech with relatively high accuracy, indicating that universal rules play a part in inferring emotions and affects from voice.

3.1.3.4 The Linguistic Domain

The linguistic domain defines an experience related to language, including verbal elements and structures from semantic to non-semantic output. As we have seen in Chap. 1, the non-semantic domain is about syllables, consonants and vowels without syntactic levels. By focusing on manipulated verbal material, phrases, words, syllables and sounds appear as sound phenomena, offering hybrid musical material oscillating between linguistic meaning and sound.

Verbal cues are deconstructed and musicalised by parametrisation of pitch, volume, duration, rhythm, tempo, density, pauses, duration changes, etc., to play a foreground role. This allows for a musical design in the vertical, i.e. the way the several layers of fictional speech-sound material sound together come to the fore, whether this is multilayered textures, rhythmic overlays or concentrated, dense polyphonic actions. In my piece *Talkings* (Fig. 3.11), I explore the vocalities of rapid speech without meaning, but with rhythmisation and vocal colouring of syllables.

Pamela Z explores in her pieces the language of asking or begging, questioning, remembering, the changing language of gender, grammar, dialect, small talk, coercion, technology and news media. She explores and sets to music the subtleties of

Fig. 3.11 *Talkings* (2022). Imaginary Music Score. *Source* © Franziska Baumann

the human speaking voice. She performs her word rituals in various roles such as narrator, news commentator, storyteller, cantor, etc. For example, in *Speech*, the audience finds itself in the midst of an acoustic and visual landscape of questions that they can answer in any way they choose, like a grammar quiz consisting entirely of trick questions.

> I love playing with that strange territory between language as meaningful communication and language as a purely sonic element. I know that if it's language that's understood by the listener, it's impossible to just throw it in there and say I'm just using it for the sound of it. So that meaning becomes a layer of the work. But you can play with things that cause that meaning to sort of recede or disappear, like repetition and layering, that will eventually make the sound start to lose its meaning in the ears of the listener. Then it will start to take on new meanings over time. (Pamela Z 2021)

Her *I was breathing* begins with a rhythmic motif on two pitches. Then she fragments and granulates syllables into particles with intrinsic sound character in terms of pitch, colour and frequency. The piece oscillates between comprehensible words of the embodied voice and pulverised, granulated, repeated and stretched letters of the mediated voice. Words become sound and conjure up a vocal sonic atmosphere, which can produce new vocal imaginative bodies.

> Sometimes it is an entire sentence, and sometimes it is just a phrase. Often it is just a single word, or even only syllables or phonemes. Then I build music out of those little building blocks. In those cases, I am taking it down to these components that begin to not mean anything specifically by themselves anymore (Pamela Z 2021).

When different kinds of electronic manipulations are used, such as filtering, time-stretching and time-compression, shuffling, etc., the semantic level of the verbal material is degraded or ambiguous. We sense speaking tubes or swarms of consonants, but the linguistic level may disappear and a new fictional linguistic field of imaginary beings may appear.

3.1.4 Persona References Conclusions

The four domains are never clearly separated and independent from each other but are mutually dependent, whereby one or the other persona reference can be in the foreground and the boundaries between them are sometimes difficult to delineate. The use of extended techniques, such as subtones, multiphonics, distorted voice, whispered voice, various ways of pressed voices, the use of falsetto, minimises the persona references and tends to fluctuate into intrinsic manifestations (Fig. 3.12).

Depending on the degree of abstraction of the vocal material by electronic modification, the persona references of the digitised voices can disappear in the human–machine interaction and/or reappear with a new meaning. A high degree of abstraction can easily cross the boundary of the concrete voice. One no longer recognises the original voice(s) as a sound source, and the references to the "persona" disappear. On this Bergsland noted:

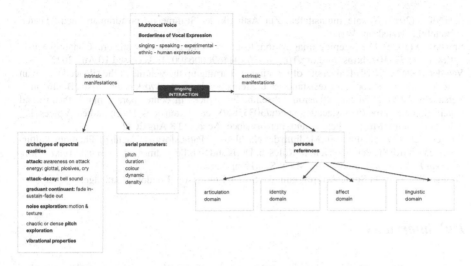

Fig. 3.12 Intrinsic and extrinsic manifestations. *Source* © Franziska Baumann

Manipulations such as filtering, time expansion or compression without pitch shifting, reverse playback, upwards and downwards shift of the pitch, granulation, shuffling and others reduce the identification of the disembodied mediated voice (Bergsland 2010).

Nevertheless, I would like to emphasise that each of the four domains can be the focus of attention and highlight meaning in relation to the others, whether the vocal utterance in question is sung, spoken, experimental, or some other vocal type.

In Chap. 1, we saw the creative potential of spectromorphological and reduced listening to musicalise the radical vocality. In this chapter, we have discussed the mediated voice as an abstract vocal terrain. In the third chapter, I will present the interplay of co-players that create meaning with gestural sensor interfaces in embodied human–computer practice.

References

Bergsland A (2010) Doctoral thesis, Norwegian University of Science and Technology. Experiencing Voice in Electroacoustic Music
Bosma H (2013) The electronic cry. Voice and Gender in Electroacoustic Music. Doctoral Thesis, Amsterdam. www.hannahbosma.nl
Drees S (2011) Körper Medien Musik, Körperdiskurse in der Musik nach 1950. Wolke Verlag, Hofheim am Taunus
Godøy RI (1997) Formalization and epistemology. Universitetsforlaget, Oslo
Hewitt DG (2006) Doctoral thesis, University of Western Sydney, Australia. Composition for Voice and Technology
Ihde D (2007) Listening and voice: phenomenologies of sound, 2nd edn. State University of New York Press, Albany, NY

Schrödl J (2012) Vokale Intensitäten: Zur Ästhetik der Stimme im postdramatischen Theater. Bielefeld, Transkript Verlag

Smalley D (1996) The listening imagination: listening in the electroacoustic era. Contemp Music Rev 13(2):77–107. https://doi.org/10.1080/07494469600640071, Accessed 10 Aug 2022

Van-der-Haar M (2020) University of Groningen. Turning up the volume of the silenced voice: an exploration of the room for resistance of the female voice in the Work of Franziska Baumann

Verstraete P (2011) Vocal extensions, disembodied voices in contemporary music theatre and performance. https://www.academia.edu/3035586/Vocal_Extensions_Disembodied_Voices_in_Contemporary_Music_Theatre_and_Performance. Accessed 8 Aug 2022

Weigel S (2006) Die Stimme als Medium des Nachlebens: Pathosformel, Nachhall, Phantom, kulturwissenschaftliche Perspektiven. In Kolesch, Doris and Sybille Krämer, eds, *Stimme: Annäherung an ein Phänomen*. Frankfurt am Main, Suhrkamp Verlag

Wishart T (1996) On Sonic Art. rev. edn, ed. Simon Emmerson. London, Routledge.

Full interviews

Nowitz A (2021) Interview. http://www.franziskabaumann.ch/en/press/interview2-nowitz.php. Accessed 12 Aug 2022

Pamela Z (2021) Interview. http://www.franziskabaumann.ch/en/press/interview1-pamela.php, Accessed Aug 2022

Listening Examples

Baumann F (2020) Re-shuffling sirenes and hunting tectonics. http://www.franziskabaumann.ch/de/solos/echoitouch, Accessed 10 Aug 2022

Baumann F (2022) Talkings. https://www.youtube.com/watch?v=xtARB9NLas0, Accessed 1 Nov 2022

Heintz J (2018) Alma. https://joachimheintz.de/reziprok.html, Accessed 10 Aug 2022

Lansky P (1985) Idle Chatter. https://www.youtube.com/watch?v=NFrtTTUsIFE, Accessed 10 Aug 2022

Norderval K (2021) Flying blind. https://vimeo.com/471932267, Accessed 10 Aug 2022

Nowitz A (2017) Mundfundstücke. https://vimeo.com/242024425, Accessed 10 Aug 2022

Nowitz A (2019) Panache. https://www.researchcatalogue.net/view/492687/492987, Accessed 10 Aug 2022

Pamela Z (2017) Span. https://vimeo.com/197703016, Accessed 10 Aug 2022

Pamela Z Speech and I was breathing. https://soundcloud.com/pamela-z, Accessed 10 Aug 2022

Chapter 4
Embodied Interface Performance with Gestural Systems

Abstract This chapter outlines a dynamic framework for creating meaningful interactions between the embodied voice and the disembodied voice through gestural systems. Based on the practices of contemporary vocal art, I will discuss the sensor instrument as prop, object and body extension and show how the sensor's functions or affordances influence mapping strategies. I will show how the composed mapping of functional and communicative gestures together with a software's logic defines a creative virtual instrument design framework. For this study, the embodied practice is presented as a dynamic system with seven co-players, a visual metaphor with seven limbs that create meaning in their interactions. To clarify this, I introduce each of these co-players separately. I present a way of understanding the creation of meaning in embodied human–computer interaction as a stream of attention with shifting perspectives. This mapping framework will be useful not only for musicians, composers and creative practitioners wishing to develop an understanding of the specifics of embodied human–computer interaction in vocal music performance but also for human–robotic researchers, voice-model and artificial machine-intelligence researchers seeking to develop a more systematic and targeted focus for exploring embodied interaction approaches in gestural systems.

4.1 Introduction

So far, I have discussed how meaning is created and communicated in the embodied and mediated voice. In this third chapter, I present the interplay of these and how they create meaning with gestural sensor interfaces in embodied human–computer practice. This interplay between different voices and agents—what I call co-players—occupy a dynamic field of meaning-making between the *first-person perspective* of the embodied voice and the *third-person perspective* of the mediated and disembodied voice (Fig. 4.1). This "in-between" *second-person perspective* embraces the communicative affect-space between the two vocal entities, where I–you relationships come alive. It consists of the several interlinked co-players as shown in Fig. 4.1.

F. Baumann, *Embodied Human—Computer Interaction in Vocal Music Performance*, SpringerBriefs in Cultural Computing, https://doi.org/10.1007/978-3-031-17985-3_4

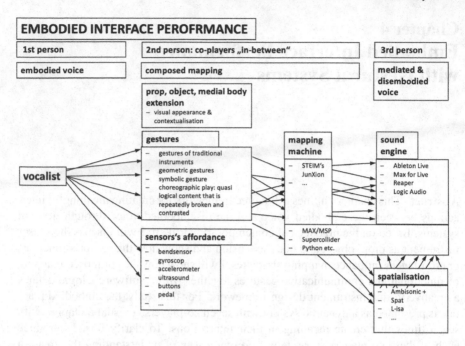

Fig. 4.1 Embodied interface performance. *Source* © Franziska Baumann

The gestural interface between the human performer and the computer translates the incoming data into available parameters. The character of the gestures associated with the sonic result refers to an embodied meaning. The design of the instrument defines a symbolic control of embodied activity. Based on the concepts of the embodied *multivocal voice* and disembodied *radical vocality*, I will discuss the sensor instrument as prop, object and body extension, and show how the sensor's affordances or functionality influence mapping strategies.

In addition to the gestures required by the technical properties of the sensors and the inherent logic of networked software, the performers engage in gestural systems with an emotional and physical presence. The body is the medium through which vocalists sound and realise musical ideas and emotions. Their body is both the emotion and the carrier of sound and musical ideas. Based on individual experiences, they develop functional and communicative gestures that define a highly personal practice. Therefore, specific intention in the mapping strategies highlights a unique body language and performance practice. This interplay of instrument design, body presence and mapping strategies holds great potential for creativity.

There is a great deal of literature on gesture system design, but literature on the long-standing use of these systems by vocalists has thus far been sparse. Based on my own experience and the insights I have gained about the work of the four fascinating artists I have interviewed—Pamela Z, Kristin Norderval, Alex Nowitz and Atau Tanaka—I will highlight some of the essential perspectives of the vocal, technical and phenomenological aspects which co-create meaning in embodied gestural interface performance. To illustrate this, I will introduce a visual metaphor, a dynamic system with seven co-players that create meaning in their interactions. I will discuss the vocalist's instrument design and how sensor affordance, self-direction, and felt-sense support expressive embodied human–computer language. Just as speakers in their native language can develop and understand an infinite number of sentences based on rules, in embodied human–machine interaction meaning and sense emerge through the way individual co-players interact.

4.2 The Interface as a Blackbox "In-Between" Vocal Entities

Before I look at the co-players of meaning generation in detail, I would like to take a look at what makes an interface alive and highlight the critical aspect of a lack of haptic feedback control in sensor interface applications.

What is an interface, and what brings it alive? A digital interface is an invisible virtual interaction space. There is an action on one side and an effect on the other. Between the two, there is a "Blackbox" that represents a reduction of available parameters to provide a manageable means of accessing the world that is "on the other side" of the interface boundary (Brandtsegg 2020).

A more metaphorical approach can be applied to sensor interfaces in the sense that technology as a necessary and creative mediation can be considered a source of ideas itself rather than merely a means for their transmission (Mudd 2019).

Since about 2010, reflection on the technological media and their cultural and social connotations has itself often been made the content. Self-referentially, media became content. But, as Alexander Schubert says, the use of electronic tools and representations today can no longer be an end in itself. Digital media has influenced our perception in such a way that not using them in an artistic work can only be a conscious decision (Schubert 2021). Dourish draws upon Heidegger's philosophy of phenomenology to ask whether interfaces are the object of attention or whether they become the transparent means of facilitating an interaction (Dourish 2004). As a result, the mediating artefact or prop comes to the fore. Palombini for example disagrees with the view of technology as a neutral tool:

> We are delivered over technology in the worst possible way when we regard it as neutral; for this conception of it, to which today we particularly like to do homage, makes us utterly blind to the essence of technology (Palombini 1998).

In other words, every technological tool has an implicit affordance and idiosyncratic use. Controlling the volume with a fader and gesticulating wildly with a gyroscope, for example, are not the same thing. The actions and gestural choices of the performer in an interactive vocal music performance should be understood as also embracing the human use of the material components of the technology.

If we use sensors to define the interaction between the incoming and outcoming data, we can connect every possible movement to every possible sound because electricity is used as an interface technology. This is significantly different from using a physical interface, as is the case with conventional musical instruments, which obey the physical laws of kinetic energy converted into sound.

Traditional instrument design is concerned with the quality of sound. This is most obvious in acoustic instruments whose shape directly affects the sound output. The interface by itself is not the instrument because it doesn't sound by itself; it is only when it is coupled to electronic modification or a sound engine. The totality of the three elements of gesture, mapping design and sonic correlation makes it an instrument. The interface is thus a fiction, a conscious playing with the imagination, the illusion of the content-related and technical processes hidden behind it. As Magnusson says: "we can state that the electronic or digital instrument has an interface, whereas the instrument is the interface" (Magnusson 2019).

In gesture-based interfaces presented in this book, vocalists use sensors designed mainly for automation in machines or measurements of all kinds. These sensors translate incoming sensed signals into a stream of data. The data is always the same. For example, if I use an ultrasound distance sensor, the sensor always sends the same data at the same location. It's not like a cello, where the pressure and the speed of the bow cause a change in the sound.

The mapping of the sensor data—itself a composition—translates gestures and applies a musical idea to the corresponding data stream. The selected translation in the mapping strategies creates new gesture phenomena and dimensions in meaning-making and, therefore, doesn't fit into traditional *organology* (Magnusson 2019). The choice of sensors and what movements they interpret, how they physically function, what vocal events they feed into a digital process and how the resulting disembodied vocal events are re-embodied leads to a unique interplay.

As a vocalist playing with a gestural system, I *am* an interface, and I *have* an interface. The voice sets the air vibrating and produces sounds. The body sounds, the vocal folds are exciters, the vocal tract amplifiers and the nasal cavities resonators. My body acts as a resonating instrument, an interface of my voice. I can vary the vocal sound, technique and content, but the body source with its individual dimensions of bones, vocal cords, resonant cavities, etc., remains the same.

In the case of the mediated voice, the sounds are removed from their source. The interface has the possibility to reconnect the disembodied voice with the body of the performer. To bring an interface to life, therefore, performers use mapping composition to create new individual body signatures with the machine. In this intermediate field, an embodied practice with the machine unfolds.

4.3 Practising Gestural Systems Without Haptic Feedback Control

A quick look at conventional instruments shows that lips, hands and fingers are the most sensitive parts of the body for exercising control and developing an acute sense of physical control. "Through direct physical contact or physical intimacy, the musician gets used to the vibrations of the musical instrument pre-reflexively, i.e. before the conscious perception of his/her body, and thereby reaches a kind of co-resonance of his/her own body, which essentially determines the feeling of making music" (Kim 2010).

In interactive live-electronic settings, the sound is basically controlled by hearing via loudspeakers and seeing via screens. The haptic sensation of a piano key is different from that of a button. One can talk about a shift of physical control and feedback parameters in interface applications (Baumann 2010).

Despite the almost unlimited potential of a gestural interface application, one essential information key is missing: the feedback of an immediate haptic body sensation. Sensors such as flexors, gyroscopes, accelerometers, infrared and ultrasound distance meters do not provide haptic feedback. In gestural systems, the physical energy of a movement can be converted into electrical currents, which in turn can be converted into digital signals. The control commands obtained in this way can be bundled. The corresponding interfaces enable entire networks of program-controlled dependencies between signal control groups and digital settings for sound generation and modification. For example, a slight finger movement can transmit a multilayered number of control signals to the live electronics—with correspondingly complex musical consequences. The acoustic energy of the resulting sound is detached from the kinetic energy of the playing movement. It has to be composed and practised on a meta-level.

Figure 4.2 represents a basic illustration of human–computer interaction with gestural systems. It shows that a composed gesture–sound interaction triggers a sensory perception in our body. On the other hand, a movement generates real information for a sensor that can be transformed into a sonic result. As we will see later, vocalists with gestural systems use multiple proprioceptive perceptions to orient themselves in this human–machine interaction. Through practice, they develop memory and felt sense for movement patterns and a body-guided purpose of transmitting expressive tension. If the felt sense is already incorporated in the mapping composition, i.e. if we *feel* how sensors are linked to sound modulations, the interaction between human and computer as shown in Fig. 4.2 can generate a higher intensity in meaning, not only for the audience but also for the performer.

Certain sensors, such as the knob, allow resistance during operation. This simplifies the control. It makes a difference whether a button has an integrated click or not. Kristin Norderval regrets a lack of "click" feeling in the buttons of her user interface:

The keys of the Genki Wave Ring lack the feeling of touch. There are no *real* buttons. So sometimes I have to steer with my eyes. There is no feeling for the click. It would be good to have a better distinction between the three buttons of the Wave Ring (Norderval 2021).

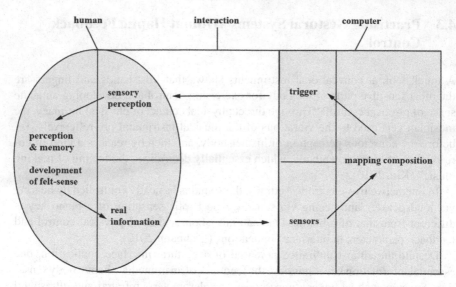

Fig. 4.2 Human–computer interaction without haptic feedback. *Source* © Baumann Franziska

Atau Tanaka realised that he needed some resistance to create muscle tension for his first instrument, the BioMuse:

> It is tricky if you don't have a string to push your finger on [...]. A concept that I developed was called the "boundary object". In some of my early BioMuse performances, even though I was waving my arms in midair, I used a rubber ball in my hands to give resistance, so my muscle had something to act on. It's not haptic feedback in a technological sense. But it's haptic feedback in the proprioceptive sense where the object is a boundary (Tanaka 2022).

How do we performers deal with the lack of feedback? Are there other aspects that give us a sense of digital transmission in music performance? Mark Johnson states that: "The meaning in and of the music is not verbal or linguistic, but rather bodily and felt. It is enacted via our active engagement with music" (Johnson 2007). Antonio Damasio (2003) says that this kind of meaning consists of a series of interrelated, interwoven patterns of neural activation. These result from an ongoing interaction between organism and environment, including various forms of sensory perception: touch, muscle, temperature, pain, visceral and vestibular. In practice, this means that vocalists with gestural systems use multiple proprioceptive perceptions to orient themselves in this human–machine interaction. I like to compare my work with gestural systems to that of a dancer who develops a kinaesthetic sense in order to develop a felt-sense of the movement patterns. Dancers also have no haptic feedback and yet develop a deep body-routed sense of the transmission of expressive tension. Mary Mainsbridge says:

> When vocalists directly engage in design, their gestural system and instruments can be informed by their musical performance experiences and reflection on the felt dimension, leading to more nuanced work (Mainsbridge 2022).

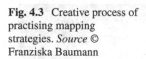

Fig. 4.3 Creative process of practising mapping strategies. *Source* © Franziska Baumann

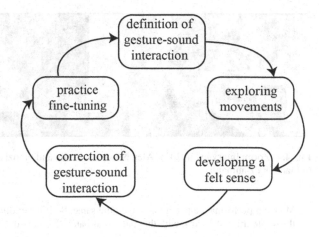

Physically experimenting with a movement-based system allows performers to develop an understanding of its implications—the changes in the mindset and the sensibility of the artists as they put it to use (Wechsler 2006). Therefore, playing with gestural interfaces needs to be practised. This is not only so that we get to know all the technical sources of error and possible crashes, but also to get an intuitive body feeling for the body-sound movements.

Figure 4.3 shows a cycle for a possible creative process to achieve a kinaesthetic sense for composing movement patterns. We define a gesture-sound interaction with the sensors, explore the movement and develop a felt sense for it. By then analysing the experience with the technical-bodily connection, we can adapt and refine the practice according to the original idea for the mapping composition, and then begin the next cycle.

Exploring movement vocabularies emerging from gesture–sound interactions leads to increased felt-sensation and a deeply routed proprioception, a kinaesthetic felt-sense for specific connections, even without haptic feedback. The feedback loop created by self-referential physicality and auditory phenomena forms a *techno-somatic* link (Mainsbridge 2022) that informs and shapes both elements it connects, performer and technological mediation. Through awareness and sensitivity to the potential and latent impact of the relationship between corporeality and technology, a kinaesthetic felt-sense can be developed.

> Through practice or rehearsal, a performer's own expressive repertoire becomes intuitive or semi-automatic […]. Levels of intuitiveness in a musical interface are also measured by how natural the control of gestures feels (Mainsbridge 2022).

Performers have developed different strategies to be able to perform in human–machine interaction. To create a flexible instrument that imposes minimal constraints on the performer, Kristin Norderval relies on a fixed patch that can navigate through the timbres and explore the possibilities of delay. It also allows her to perform without visual feedback and to sing without amplification.

Fig. 4.4 Zoom Interview in 2021: Alex Nowitz in Berlin and Franziska Baumann in Berne. *Source* © Franziska Baumann

> My main performance patch has stayed the same. So it is building each piece, not building the whole thing if I work with that particular patch (Norderval 2021).

The advantage is also that we do not have to update systems all the time. As Pamela Z explains:

> What if you were a cellist and you had a 200-year-old instrument, and you were playing that instrument for a long time, and you have become virtuosic on that instrument. What if every six months somebody comes to your house saying to you: I am sorry, but we don't support this cello anymore. You are going to need to play this cello 1.03. We are sorry we changed the bridge's height now, and we have added a second bow, and you have to learn to play this one because we are going to take you the old one away. It would be so frustrating (Pamela Z 2021) (Fig. 4.4).

Alex Nowitz also sees the instrumental approach as a foreground practice:

> I decided to stay with one specific set of preferences, because I am not a programmer myself, which means that I always need help if I decide to re-program the software. If you play the piano, for instance, it always works the same, too. It is the task of the musician to keep the playing of the instrument interesting and surprising. The way we play and make decisions upon the course of music is, more important than having a new set of features and control parameters available (Nowitz 2021).

The more components we want to embody and play with in gestural systems, the more complicated and technical it becomes (Fig. 4.5). With a predominantly technical focus, we lose the physical–communicative and musical meaning. We sit or stand in front of our computers and think about how to control things. According to Steven Gelineck (2012), a good system includes balancing the simplicity of controls with infinite possibilities to achieve precision, expression and exploitability. Fewer relationships between voice and vocal processes in their mutually charging interaction allow moving the practice toward a musical-driven embodied human–machine interaction. It allows the development of a deeply routed proprioceptive sense of performance. The perceived embodiment of the experience maximises the emotional and unconscious effects of the musical practice. This is where the potential lies for the flow of creative and embodied interface performance without haptic feedback.

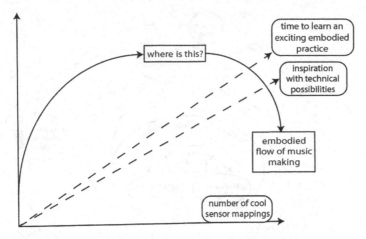

Fig. 4.5 Embodied flow of music-making. *Source* © Franziska Baumann

4.4 Co-players Creating Meaning in the Human–Computer Interaction

This section outlines a framework for identifying seven co-players surrounding the embodied and mediated voice. It presents a metaphor that illuminates multiple angles to understand how meaning is created in gestural interaction between humans and computers.

Each co-player in Fig. 4.6 can mean something in the overall piece. During a performance, the co-players and vocal content are subject to continuous change and modification. In a stream of attention, the relationship and the interplay between them play an integral role in a musical piece. Understanding the potential of each player and levels of interaction in a gestural system supports creating meaning-making in sensor interface performance.

4.4.1 The Body as Instrument

The body acts as our "anchorage" in the world and forms the basis of our communication with it (Merleau-Ponty 1999). It provides access to immediate experiences that precede reflective or critical thinking. Rather than being an object of the world, the body forms the basis of our communication with it (Merleau-Ponty 1999). Merleau-Ponty sees the body as central to our understanding and communication with the world: it forms the basis of our experience and our belonging to an environment. By placing the body and movement awareness at the centre of performance, gestural systems offer musicians a heightened sense of immediacy and immersion, allowing the body to become a conduit for sounds otherwise inaccessible (Mainsbridge 2022).

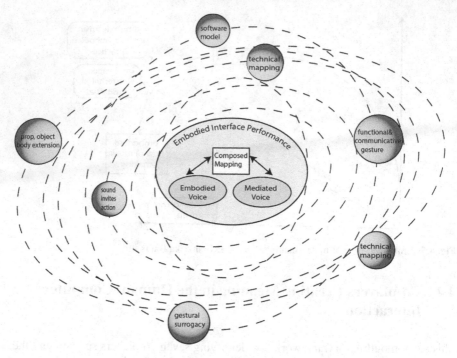

Fig. 4.6 Co-players creating meaning in their interplay. *Source* © Franziska Baumann

Mark Johnson says in his book *The Meaning of The Body*:

> A fundamental fact about music is that it appeals to our felt sense of life. Granted theorists
> can listen to music for analytical purposes, focusing on key changes, rhythm patterns, pitch
> contours, and harmonic progressions, but most of us are simply imaginatively and emotion-
> ally drawn into music, without any theoretical knowledge of what is happening. [...] The
> music is a body-mind experience, something *felt*. (Johnson 2007).

This view represents the embodied meaning I aim for in an embodied practice
with technical tools and machines when I explore music through gestures. It allows
an intuitive and emotional perception of the performance and thus opens up access
to live electronic music to a larger audience.

> An embodied view of meaning looks for the origins and structures of meaning in the
> organic activities of embodied creatures in interaction with their changing environments.
> [...] [the meanings] must be grounded in our bodily connection with things, and they must
> be continuously "in the making" via sensomotoric engagement (Johnson 2007).

The body is, therefore, our interface to grasp meaning. It is considered the most
original instrument.

However, the acquisition of meaning is not absolute but is formed by our individual perceptions and accumulated experiences. In the embodied theory of meaning,
meaning is relational. It is about how one thing relates to the other. Therefore, it is

subject to constant change, and we can continually expand our sense-making and explore new aesthetic experiences. Mary Mainsbridge notes in her book *The Body Instrument* that we can develop a felt sense adapted to the architecture of gestural systems:

> Gestural systems can establish new forms of connection between sound and body, reinforcing felt connections to bodily sensations beyond the physical constraints of a conventional instrument, which requires the body to conform to a particular design architecture (Mainsbridge 2022).

Individual approaches to gestural systems development lead to divergent priorities and criteria. It characterises an embodied interaction of the individual co-players, such as the physical behaviour of sensors, the design of the interface and its *ergodynamic* (Magnusson 2019) qualities acquired by mapping strategies and the individual gesture vocabulary.

Many vocalists who play with sensor interfaces design their instruments themselves, combining the roles of designer, researcher, programmer-cum-mapper and user. The strategies for this are individual and allow individual physicalities to emerge in the human–computer interaction. The way artists design an interface with mapping strategies significantly influences how they play it and how we perceive the sounds through the conceptual metaphor resulting from that playing of a gestural system. To compose mappings means also creating an instrument. I have the choice of whether I want to execute sample triggering or sound modifications with large or small movements, respectively a more or less expressive movement (Fig. 4.7).

Playing with Ambisonic

Ambisonic[1] is a sound design tool that turns the room into a three-dimensional instrument. I think about the placement of sounds in space to create a disembodied illusion of immersion. I simultaneously embody the spatialised vocal extensions with my gestural system. As I experience the real world three-dimensionally, the perceived "realness" with Ambisonic leads to a sense of emotional and embodied participation. Vocal sounds inhabit a much larger space, and their details can be perceived to a heightened degree. I invite the listeners to immerse themselves in the mediated voice. Ambisonic enables the creation of vocal spheres and sculptures that can evoke imaginary figures and worlds and deepen the physical experience of disembodied voices.

In my interface set-up for 3D Ambisonic diffusion, I have a virtual radar image on the screen as a reference for my spatialised vocal placements and trajectories. To play with third-order Ambisonic, I for example use the horizontal and vertical axes of the gyroscope built in my SensorGlove. With my hand up, I place the mediated voice at the front of the room, correspondingly at the back when it is down. The radar image unfolds vertically in front of me, so to speak, for which I develop a body feeling over time. In a large room, I have to slow down the speed of my gestures if I want to have a continuous spatialised movement. Otherwise, the sound flips quickly from one place to another. I need some time to adjust my body feeling with the gyroscope to the respective room and speaker placement.

When I additionally map the gyroscope with fragmentation and delay, I design vocal processing parameters for specific room placements. When the hand is up and the sound is at the front of the room, the delay is longer, the fragmentation is minimal, and correspondingly, it is maximal at the back of the room. The distance between the two hands is measured with the ultrasonic device. If I use it in addition to the above constellation to control the feedback, unforeseen combinations also arise in the constellation, which I then physically recapture. My body then re-adapts to the machine, so to say. The space becomes a further instrument where movements and acoustics are intrinsic features of vocal sound.

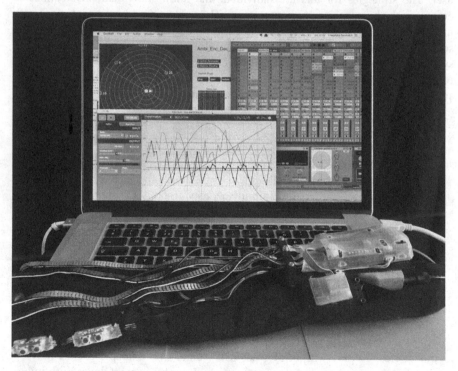

Fig. 4.7 Ambisonic radar image, software and a SensorGlove. *Source* © Franziska Baumann

---

[1] Ambisonics is a full-sphere surround sound format or a means of representing the sound field at a point or in space. Unlike conventional stereo and surround sound formats (which are based on the principle of panning audio signals to specific speakers), ambisonics captures the full directivity

Participation in movement-based electronic music requires redefined kinaesthetic awareness to improve movement expertise, reflected through enhanced movement variation, economy, and efficacy (Mainsbridge 2022).

I argue that we humans as participants in cultural activities consistently ask for meaning, and that this generation of meaning takes a central perspective. In the case of technical tools, we are inspired not only by the surfaces developed but also by the kind of embodied logic associated with them. By that, I mean that the felt-sense transmits meaning to the embodied structures we develop with mapping strategies between humans and computers.

4.4.2 Designing Sensor Interfaces as Instrument, Prop, Object or Mediated Body Extension

With each specific prop or interface, one chooses an idiosyncratic embodiment, appearance and affordance with a particular type of body image and gestural inscription. Although the mechanics of gestures, interfaces and sound engines are practically infinite, the chosen prop and software define the instrument character and the symbolic control as a source of embodied activity. As T. Mudd puts it in *Material-Oriented Musical Interaction*, this is "a more material-oriented approach, which sees technology as a necessary and creative mediation that can be a source of creativity itself than simply a means for their transmission" (Mudd 2019). A glittering SensorGlove, a Wii controller or bare hands with painted fingernails that magically surround an object with various gestures create different expectations in terms of sound-shaping.

Communication-orientated perspectives tend to foreground the agency of the human, whilst material-orientated perspectives draw attention to the agency of the technology (Mudd 2019).

The choice of the interface technology foregrounds either the material-orientated perspectives or the communication-orientated perspectives of the interaction, depending on the way it is played (Fig. 4.8).

For Atau Tanaka, he is entirely unconcerned about what the interface and he, as a performer, look like, and he tends to foreground the agency of technology and therefore the material-oriented perspectives. He states that:

There is a lot of imagination about what technology can do. And the companies that make the technology try to sell you the technology by making it look magical and easy. We know that working with technology often comes with crashes. It doesn't do what we want it to do. We struggle with it, and also, it's challenging to do anything creative and fluid with it. So why lie about it? I'm not interested in looks. I don't care if I look like Frankenstein in the biomedical case or a cyborg in the Myo case. The essential thing for me is affordability. What does the instrument offer me musically in terms of gestures? (Tanaka 2022).

---

information for every soundwave that hits the microphone. Crucially, this also includes height information, as well as the full 360° around the microphone.

Fig. 4.8 Atau Tanaka performing at STEIM Amsterdam, 2008. *Source* © Frank Baldé

My First Sensor (G)Love

When I started working with digital software in the late nineties, I recorded my own voice and composed vocal phenomena with the computer using sound processing and collage techniques. The digital processing of vocal sounds, in turn, inspired me to explore new vocal ideas. Then I was looking for a way to perform with my electrified vocal terrain on stage. But I did not want to be tied to buttons and faders at a mixing desk. I was led by the romantic idea of touching sounds in space with my fingers and playing with the body as an instrument. My hands are an extension of the voice when I sing. The gestures were there long before I used a sensor interface (Fig. 4.9).

Fig. 4.9 STEIM's SensorGlove, Franziska Baumann playing at AudioArt Festival Krakow 2005. *Source* © Andrzej Kramarz

I was obsessed with developing a haptic and kinaesthetic feeling for the mediated voice. I felt the wish to make the intangible tangible through my imagination and physical contributions to music-making and sound art. I aimed to "re-incarnate" these disembodied vocalities with my body, my sense of touch, and my gestures. I applied for a residency at STEIM (Studio for Electro-Instrumental Music) in Amsterdam in 2001. Their focus on and experience with developing electronic instruments close to the body corresponded to my vision of embodied vocal performance. In collaboration with the creative staff I developed the first SensorGlove in 2001, which allowed me to gesturally control voice, sound and spatialised vocal articulations in real-time. My partner Daniel Repond has been programming the SensorLab software in C++ for 15 years. Since 2016, Andreas Litmanowitsch in Berne has been designing my new sensor instruments, which I program using STEIM's JunXion software (Fig. 4.10).

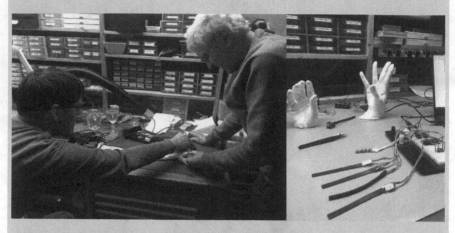

Fig. 4.10 The Electronic Design Studio with Andreas Litmanowitsch and Stefan Rothe, Berne. *Source* © Franziska Baumann

In concerts, I realised that the audience perceived my interacting as a singer with a sensor interface differently in terms of meaning. The interface itself assumed an expressive character with the cables running from the arm to the fingers. There were people who associated the glove with hospital technology, others with cyber technology, others with digital sound dance, and so on.

The SensorGlove, the Wave Rings, the Strophonion, a sensor board worn directly on the wrist, and the Myo armband are interfaces that each offer the performer a slightly different character of embodied communication. My SensorGlove, with its exposed cables that reach from the fingers to the end of the arm, has some kind of a vintage character. We all know electricity, and that's why the glove is a prop reminiscent of electrical devices. It attracts attention and people want to know how it works. Together with my gestural language, the glove allows the development of an individualised performative identity through technology.

Kristin Norderval's performance with the wireless Wave Rings, barely visible from afar, foregrounds the agency of the human. We don't see any technical equipment in her performance area and therefore experience her interface as an extension of the body. In terms of the invisibility of the interface, Marie Mainsbridge says:

Compared to instrumental and laptop performances, which elevate the utility of objects as supportive props, audience expectations are projected directly onto the performer's body when the instrument is largely invisible (Mainsbridge 2022).

Fig. 4.11 Pamela Z presenting mass control in our Zoom interview, 2021. *Source* © Franziska Baumann

In the *Typewriter Song*, Pamela Z plays with a wireless sensor board on her wrist. The typing movements create the sound of an old typewriter. Her fingers tap the air and produce recognisable, realistic typing sounds with a carriage return sound when she pulls her right hand to the left. We know this type of sound control from our everyday experience and thereby her wireless sensor board becomes an object character.

In another piece, she plays with a standalone sensor object that has an inbuilt mass sensor (Fig. 4.11). Her subtle gestures make one think of concrete material processing, such as kneading. I know of no analogue instrument that is played with kneading movements. Soft material usually sounds quiet because it cannot produce standing vibrations. The way she plays with the mass sensor creates an idiosyncratic movement that develops its own logic together with the sound samples. Together with her communication-oriented gestures, this sensor brings the characteristics of a virtual instrument to the fore.

Alex Nowitz, a trained pianist, has developed a sensor instrument called the Strophonion that is equipped with many keys:

> First of all, there is an instrument approach to the Strophonion. To put it simply, there are twelve buttons to playback samples within the range of a whole octave. This octave, of course, can be transposed. In this sense the Strophonion works in a traditional way (Nowitz 2021).

But when he starts sampling his voice, the Strophonion reveals a completely different approach. The movements of his arms, indeed of his whole body, become a sound dance that goes beyond the controller function of the wooden objects in his hands. The Strophonion mutates from an instrument into a body extension.

The way *ergodynamic* (Magnusson 2019) qualities interact with mediating artefacts can change the perception of the interface as an instrument, prop, object or body extension. Whether an interface is an object, an interface with prop characteristics or a body extension depends mostly on how we play with it. For example, the same interface can have both communication-oriented perspectives that foreground the agency of humans and material-oriented perspectives that foreground the agency of technology. The type of gestural mediation in the interaction process of body, sound

Fig. 4.12 Zoom Interview in 2021: Kristin Norderval in Oslo and Franziska Baumann in Berne. *Source* © Franziska Baumann

and technology changes the respective focus and thus the perception of the interface itself.

A high degree of personalisation and customisation in gesture interface design allows musicians to define their gesture vocabulary. They can define gestures that feel personally natural for the musical action.

> With each piece, I have to make a decision on which gestures control which sound manipulation. Often, I have to think about the easiest and the most comfortable way and what feels the most natural to produce a specific sound (Pamela Z 2021).

Alex Nowitz combines the same gestures with the same controllers in his compositions. In this way, he creates meaning, recognisability and comprehensibility as he understands his Strophonion as an instrument:

> I decided to stay with one set of preferences instead of re-defining the instrument every time I present a new piece. For instance, if you play the piano, it always works the same, too. (Nowitz 2021).

Kristin Norderval says about the wireless Wave Ring:

> It is a body extension because I am not thinking of it as an object. I don't have to hold it. I mean, it is an object. Maybe it feels like jewellery. I put in the programme notes that I am controlling with the wireless mid-ring. So I am not trying to hide that from the audience, but I like that it is not specific to anything in the high-tech world (Norderval 2021).

With the digital sensor interface, I design an instrument. The way it looks defines the symbolic control of embodied activity. "If she is wearing a SensorGlove, she must be able to control something," people say. But in contrast to a traditional instrument like a piano, they don't know its range of potential sounds, mutations and so on (Fig. 4.12).

4.4.3 Playing with the Sensor's Technical Potential and Expressiveness

This section explores the technical-oriented perspective of sensors and the inherent agency they provide. Musicians usually have their gestural systems built with sensors that already exist. They use sensors to build body-related instruments such as gloves, wearable hand instruments, finger rings and standalone sensor objects. As users of existing tools, they have to deal with their traditional logic and idiosyncrasies. The intrinsic features provide specific conditions for the qualities of gesture mapping.

The sensor objects allow the body to articulate energy in a more or less visible way. Artists compose with or for these sensors. In contrast to a traditional instrument, they use them to build their *ergonomics* individually.

The sensor technology itself is direct since a sensor always delivers precisely the same data in the course of the same movement. This information can be used to control countless different options. Therefore, sensor interfaces are entirely freed from the limitations of traditional instruments because the physical laws that force a particular gesture to produce a specific sound no longer exist.

Nevertheless, each sensor has a specific characteristic, a way of "sensing" the real world and of recognising physical or chemical properties. And each sensor asks for the corresponding movement to utilise the sensor qualities optimally.

The sensors themselves lead to a certain movement vocabulary through their inherent physical properties (Fig. 4.13). If I assign the same functions to different sensors, I get different sound results. For example, if I trigger precomposed samples on a horizontal movement on the x-axis of a gyro sensor, I must first set a virtual grid that determines the number of triggers. This results in a "scanning the space" gesture because I don't have haptic feedback or an absolute felt-sense for the number of events I'm triggering on the horizontal axis.

If, on the other hand, I use an accelerator for the same function, I first create a list of clips to be played. With a separate button, I go back and forth through this list. Then I decide in which direction the accelerator should trigger the sound with a "tap" in the air—inwards, outwards, upwards or downwards. The two gestures make the resulting experience sound differently.

Atau Tanaka has long-standing research experience with sensors. He says:

> The sensors themselves have affordances. The bricolage and the assemblages of sensors that we build as instruments will have their meta-affordances and our bodies perform them and

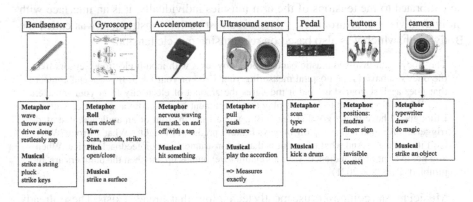

Fig. 4.13 Sensors and their expressiveness. *Source* © Franziska Baumann

are invited to create different kinds of gestures that are appropriate for the sensors, that allow each sensor to articulate in a way that best articulates here (Tanaka 2022).

Pamela Z explains that one of her sensors—which controls mass—has led her to more subtle movements:

> You need to have some subtlety in your movement to draw more subtle things out of the mass controller. Playing them just trained me to have this more fluent and subtle movement. The practice with mass control changed the quality of my gestures (Pamela Z 2021).

Kristin Norderval's research approach with interactive gestural systems focuses on playing without visual feedback. The gyroscopes built into the wireless Genki Wave Ring allow her to play her live recorded voice using three buffers, feedback and delay with just a few movements of the right and left arms. With the simplicity of gestural connections, she searches for the most adequate embodiment of it. Her right hand is the functional and structuring conductor, and her left hand is more the shaping, varying conductor.

> It was just exploring which sensor I want to use for feedback and which one for the delay [...] That very simple mapping becomes much more complicated because it means listening all the time, and you get all these coincidental overlays and folding (Norderval 2021).

Another interesting aspect is that she assigns the speakers directly according to the arrangement of the keys on the right Wave Ring. Thus, she has a physical reference to the placement of the speakers in the room.

In contrast to sensor systems, Tanaka's electromyogram–muscle interaction no longer separates the body and the human performer from the interface. In his embodied practice, the muscle tension creates voltage differences and this can be assigned to any controlling function.

> Muscle sensing is interesting because you need to activate the muscles to make a movement. It's not the result of musical action, it's the intention of musical expression. We pick up musical gestures with electromyogram sensing before movement happens. (Tanaka 2022).

The intention of musical expression is linked directly to the body. As it has to be calibrated to the tensions of the arm muscles individually, it is an interface with individual visceral affordances. Pamela Z's first gestural instrument was called the BodySynth, which was also based on recognising muscle tension:

> The BodySynth involved elastic bands around my arms with inbuilt electrode sensors like the ones you have in the hospital measuring your EKG or your EEG. It is a metal contact that goes against your skin, and it measures the amount of electricity from your muscle. [...] When I first started to learn to play that instrument in my studio and practice with it, I thought: "I have to get good at this." But, when I got in front of an audience, it started triggering like mad and going off in ways I didn't predict. I thought: "What's wrong? Why isn't it working?" And what turns out is that this instrument is a biofeedback device. When you get in front of an audience, your adrenalin level bumps up and then the numbers are all jumbled (Pamela Z 2021).

Musicians and composers use mostly technology that already exists. These already existing sensors invite actions, gestures and movements that arise from their inherent technical possibilities. The required motion may result in more or less physical expressivity, such as in the accelerometer, which requires acceleration to trigger the desired data. With the gyroscope, I can determine the range of horizontal and vertical movements in calibrated tables.

> These sensor instruments are, in a sense, the most natural extension of the body. Both in a phenomenological sense and a media sense, it seems. In Merleau-Ponty's phenomenology, the blind man's cane is an extension, and at the tip of the stick, the blind man sees. Then in Marshall McLuhan's media theory, we build technologies that are the *extensions of man*. We build the tools, and the tools build us (Tanaka 2022).

With regard to the limitations and possibilities that the sensors offer us, we develop individual approaches in the gesture-finding process. We build an idiosyncratic body practice that we communicate through vocal sounds. Our movement preferences coordinate with a more or less flexible technological situation by means of empirical practice. To a not inconsiderable extent, the sensors allow limited variations of how we can create mappings. But it is then up to us if we decide to assign outdated and dismantled social conventions to the gesture system or if we re-imagine new connections and performative identities with an enlarged gestural vocabulary.

> It's about understanding the character of the device and composing for it. I think that is a "respect" for the object. We are in technology and engineering. We usually try to create an ideal situation that doesn't usually exist, but we try to solve all the problems and create something perfect. On the other hand, there is no such thing as "perfect" in music. Music is created because we try to work with the imperfect (Tanaka 2022).

One could compare the problem with the characteristics and immanent limitations of sensors with those of instruments. A violin is not a saxophone and is certainly not a drum-kit. In order to write a melody, a rhythm or a sonic idea, one needs corresponding compositional skill. It is a matter of moving from the extended sound-gesture imagination to the idiomatic handling of sensors, similar to instrumental skill. Within the struggle that comes with customising imperfect machines, I recognise opportunities for me as a composer as they transform my compositional approaches. I build a gestural system that finally builds me as well. The willingness to explore sensory modalities in human–computer interaction enhances the sensitivity and expressiveness of musicians in live electronic performances.

4.4.4 Software as a Model of Logic

The software is a model of how we can think about processes. Not all musicians are talented programmers. The selected software predetermines the musical output for the compositional process using mapping strategies. Depending on the software, the same idea has to be realised differently. Whether a musician uses MAX/MSP, Supercollider or similar software to build the whole surface from scratch, or composes with standardised software like Ableton, Reaper or Logic Audio, each method requires a different technical organisation. It chooses a lens with a specific potential outcome based on the features of the software or programming language and its predefined technical agencies. It defines a topology of thinking processes in embodied human–computer interaction as a model of how composition and interactive processes can be organised, based on the organology of how sonic interaction can be played, including options and restraints. For example, it is easy to play chord progressions with a guitar but not so easy to play sustained notes.

When creating mapping strategies with specific programs, forms of interaction emerge that imply affordances. Over time we internalise the software interface and the sensor's affordances and can anticipate the possible interface links imaginatively. This imaginative connection with the digitally possible processes is essential for creative work with mapping strategies.

4.4.5 Parametric Mapping Strategies

Four different theoretical approaches describe mapping strategies between sensor data and control parameters (Fig. 4.14, 4.15, 4.16 and 4.17). The greater the complexity in embodied interaction relationships, the less accurately one can predict how the whole will sound. Composing and playing in a digital realm differs from composing and playing with a traditional instrument, because digital instruments represent sound and movement as numbers.

Typical musical instruments function like the fourth variant (Fig. 4.17): multidimensional gestures control many output parameters. Where is the volume control on the violin? Volume is controlled by coordinating bow pressure and speed, string choice, finger position and so on. The coordinating function of the body can control multidimensional parameters in a sonically sophisticated way. These multidimensional constellations of parameter assignments create a dilemma with gestural systems. The more diverse the technically controllable parameters are, the more fragile the systems become with regard to their embodied musical engagement. Our sense of sight is too slow to immediately and intuitively shape screen information

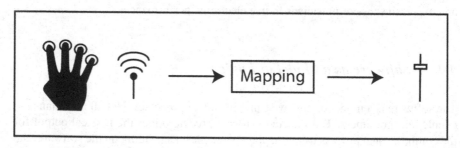

Fig. 4.14 One-to-one relationships: fixed assignments of control and result are designed one-dimensionally. *Source* © Franziska Baumann

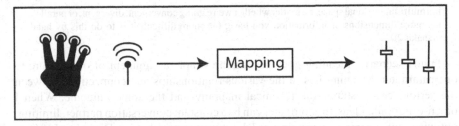

Fig. 4.15 Diverging: one gesture is assigned to several parameters; a single input splits into a multitude of outputs. *Source* © Franziska Baumann

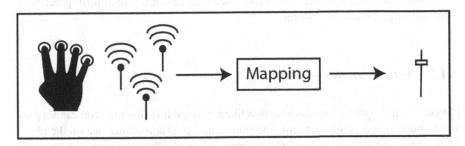

Fig. 4.16 Converging: many gestures are assigned to one parameter; the multidimensional input is mapped to one output parameter. *Source* © Franziska Baumann

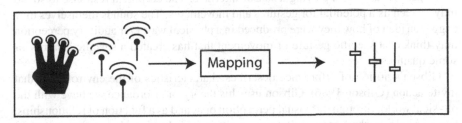

Fig. 4.17 Multidimensional relationships: many gestures control many output parameters. *Source* © Franziska Baumann

gesturally and musically. It takes a lot of practice and recurrent fine-tuning to play with several parameters simultaneously. They may behave in unexpected ways.

For example, if I flex the bend sensors for volume control, simultaneously measure the distance between my hands using ultrasound for feedback variations, while the gyroscope controls the horizontal and vertical axes in space, unpredictable combinations of sound may arise. Mapping is the link between the physical and sonic world. The various behaviours arising from multiple combinations challenge the creative collaboration between me as a performer and the computer.

Atau Tanaka believes that the simple case is communicative and powerful, because:

in a multidimensional space, no matter whether we're going convergent, divergent, or parallel, the more dimensions of information you have, the more difficult it is to do this by hand (Tanaka 2022).

In this scenario, meaning goes beyond the simple assignment of one gesture to one parameter. Meaning lies in the various relationships and connections between the performer's gestures, the technical mapping and the sonic outcome. When I practise mapping ideas, the computer can be a constant conversation partner, limiting, outlining, constraining, expressing and deforming musical ideas. Digital technology can be a much more active participant in creating meaning in a series of complex relationships based on simple mapping ideas. And it is in these relationships that the meaning of the game lies. Therefore, meaning lies in the relationship between combinations of creative gestures.

4.4.6   Sound Invites Action

Physical sound control does not function like a musical instrument: "You cannot play a soft sound when you hit a drum, and you cannot play something fast on the piano by moving your fingers slowly" (Harenberg 2010). Because the physical laws that force a particular gesture to produce a specific sound do not exist when using a sensor interface, we need to examine the ways that sound invites action, and what gestures do to the performer who is playing a sensor interface. The corporeal response to sound may be seen as a potential for gestures and movements. The sounds themselves may trigger an idea of how they were produced in a physical way. Our auditory perception may think of a specific gesture or movement that has created a specific sonority or sonic qualities.

Gibson's notion of affordance describes characteristics of the environment that invite action (Gibson 1986). Gibson uses his theory of affordance we have with the physical world, through our visual perception of it, and as a function of relationships. For example, a chair may invite you to sit on it. Likewise, the acoustic–musical experience and regular contact with the objects surrounding us help us establish a relationship between the material and the type of gesture that can produce the specific sound of that material. This experience allows us to establish patterns and relationships between the sound and the related material that makes it. For example, if someone rolls a pencil on a table instead of hitting it, the resulting sound will most likely be quieter. The faster a movement is done, the louder the sounding result. Applause would be very quiet if everyone in the audience made slow clapping movements. In this sense, loud sounds may invite fast action.

Unlike musical instruments, everyday objects do not usually allow for sophisticated sound results. For this reason, musical instruments do not always meet our typical expectations of the sounds they can produce with a gesture. Or, in other words, the sound experienced musicians can produce with an instrument often exceeds what we can imagine with ordinary objects. Therefore, like gestural systems, they too can sometimes create an almost magical relationship between gesture and sound. An instrument-specific repertoire of gestures makes the resulting sound more or less visible. For example, the dynamics of a percussionist are more visible than those of a trumpeter. The intensity of a timbre can be visually conveyed more powerfully by the bowing gesture of a double bass player than by the blowing of a woodwind player.

Considering that each person has a different relationship with their body, and a different relationship of that body to the outside world (Tanaka 2019), it is inevitable that the strategies with which we control our bodies in physical activity are highly personal. The way sound invites action must therefore rely also upon the individual, and what they perceive as meaningful gesture. Atau Tanaka says that sounds can follow a particular morphology:

> The fact that I'm working with muscle, the interaction does change the kinds of sounds I compose as a musician because there are certain kinds of sounds that I find appropriate or that I feel viscerally coherent or somehow meaningful. And these sounds are sounds that can follow a particular morphology—to recall Dennis Smalley's notion of spectromorphology. They are continuous sounds that can be sculpted because the kinds of musical gestures that I make almost shape physical gestures (Tanaka 2022).

The nature of the embodied action combined with the corresponding sound creates a unique meaning. The closer the resulting sounds in human–computer interaction can be associated with the embodied actions, the higher the intensity of the meaning generated.

The activeness of gestures invited by the sound, together with breathing and singing, flows from us to the audience and results in experiences of embodied sharing. It invites the audience to be intensely engaged in a musical process with their visual, kinaesthetic and auditory senses.

4.4.7 Gestures: Complementary and Communicative

Moving in a sound-oriented rather than choreographic way may take advantage of our intuitive associations between sound and physical movement. Godøy refers to the gestures that musicians make spontaneously as ancillary gestures, "shaping the performance on a higher level of motor control and musical intention" (Godøy 2006).

Luke Windsor categorises musical actions in traditional instrumental playing in two ways, according to their relative importance for sound production. Firstly, they directly produce sounds or indirectly influence sound production or, secondly, they complement sound production. The second category includes cyclical movements such as tapping the feet, nodding the head or swinging the body, which is phase-coupled with the beat or barre or is related to tempo changes, dynamic shaping or the like. These movements are not necessary to produce a sound. It is possible to play a woodwind instrument without making movements of the upper body that would be visible to a distant observer. The lungs must be filled and emptied, and the fingers must operate the mechanism of the keys, but the visible swaying of a body and the resulting movement of an entire instrument is not a direct source of the sound (Windsor 2011).

We can call these ancillary gestures complementary or communicative gestures. Being inwardly moved by the sound may produce movements in the performer that are not at all necessary for making the sound. However, they increase the intensity of perception for the listener and the performer. The instantaneity of a musical action involves the body in an immediate presence. The underlying "unnecessary movements" may foster the experience of sensory appreciation to pursue a more satisfying or exciting experience through the enhanced engagement of the body. Alex Nowitz says:

> Once you allow happening that your senses, as a musician, open up to the whole body, you also gain a deeper understanding of the meaning of the gestures you apply. After sharpening my awareness of whole-body movements, I realised that I finally understood much better the claim of my practice (Nowitz 2021).

Moving in the Music

Engaging physically–gesturally, I raise my felt-sense as a performer. I enter into a whole-body experience with the sonic world and the communication of musical ideas. These qualities only come into play once I have practised and embodied the mapping compositions. A felt-sense for the agency of the sensors associated with the action and its parametric mapping strategy in relation to the logic of the software gives a sense of control. I can then move more freely in the music, resulting in a sense of pleasure and reward. These feelings can encourage deep immersion and empowerment through music-making.

The communicative aspect of these movements is how these qualities of movements are felt and experienced by us. It is about how our bodies are inhabited during a performance and interact meaningfully within a performance beneath a level of conscious awareness. The specific energetic tension in the body transfers to the audience. I want to suggest that even at these subconscious levels, these movements are forming the basis for meaning-making in embodied interface performance.

Learning to move in a new way with gestural systems can overcome certain persona references—discussed in Chap. 2—of the natural, embodied voice and signal even more profound empowerment that changes the singer's self-understanding and expands their expressive potential. As Mary Mainsbridge says:

> Performers can explore and undermine the cultural connotations associated with the voice, signified by markers of gender, race, ethnicity, and history, reimaging their sonic imprint in relation to movement and sound with the aid of gestural systems (Mainsbridge 2022).

Based on individual experiences, performers develop movement patterns defining a highly personal practice. We compose the music we feel and practise gesturally in human–computer interaction, exploring new organology between the embodied and the disembodied voice. Therefore, the communicative aspects of gesture-mediated music co-shape the creative act of meaning-making.

In human–computer interaction, here is a sort of freedom to how we interpret vocal sounds and their sonic modifications, on how gestures produce vocal phenomena, so to say. Therefore, we constantly reorganise what we see and what we hear.

4.4.8 Gestural Surrogacy and Symbolic Interaction

Gestural systems allow performers to convey far more than purely numerical connections between the sensor and the digital output. Through physical engagement, emotional, theatrical and performative intentions can be made visible and experienced. Movement can become the object of design in gestural surrogacy or symbolic interaction. In contrast to communicative or complementary gestures, the performers design their gesture assignments intentionally. Such designed actions established through felt-sense can contribute significantly to finding satisfying meanings in the gestural communication of embodied and disembodied voices. Pieter Verstraete juxtaposes Alex Nowitz's approach with mine:

> Baumann seems to control the feedback with a gentle hand. The data glove gives her control over a wide range of sound parameters, with some of her gestures seemingly added purely for dramatic effect. Nowitz's rapid movement of the controllers also emphasises the control aspect. Yet, with his often almost robotic movements, he is sometimes reminiscent of a puppeteer or juggler—as if he is trying to direct the invisible sounds into a concrete space in front of him that he can control. According to the principle of reciprocity, Nowitz thus permanently tests the location of his disembodied vocal sounds, which he positions and distorts as auditory self-images and repeatedly covers with new disembodied sounds (Verstraete 2015).

With gestural surrogacy, performers not only design a specific gesture associated with a sound modification but open up a specific aura of intention with which the singer–performer can choose the concept for the movement. The singer's use of movement extends the technical possibilities into a theatrical and symbolic dimension.

The question arises of how the movements of traditional musical instruments and everyday objects may influence the mapping assignment of gestures to digital interfaces. The musical background and the daily experience with the objects that surround us help to establish connections between physical materials and the types of gestures that will produce specific sounds with those materials. Through our experience, we establish patterns and links between sonic events and the materials that could produce these sounds.

However, the perception of these relations is not always precise. For example, it is difficult to predict how loud the sound of this book being dropped to the floor might be. But in relative terms, I can definitely say that the sound of this book being dropped to the floor is a different sound than the sound of this book being torn to pieces.

Assuming I wanted to trigger the sound of the falling book with a sensor gesture, I would need a concept for the gesture to play the sound with. Do I borrow the gesture from instrumental gestures, meta-gestures, a geometric movement or a choreographic combination of all? What does it mean for the conceptual design of embodied scenarios with sensor interfaces? What metaphors can we draw on to clarify, classify and expand our gesture vocabulary? And what kind of body images do we transfer with gestural systems?

Answering these questions requires the exploration of possible concepts of gestural interaction between our mostly unconscious experience of embodied meaning and disembodied vocal actions. Finally, we need to recognise how the bodily basis of meaning leads us to a new understanding of symbolic interaction that challenges our most cherished assumptions about traditional connections between body and sound. What we see and hear in performances with gestural interfaces is no longer based on the traditional association of sound and kinetic energy.

This leads us to a taxonomy of gestural surrogacy in embodied interface performance.

We can establish five movement concepts in gestural surrogacy.

1. **Gestural Concepts of Acoustic Instruments**

   Any of the objects around us would allow the production of similarly amazing sounds as the ones made by a musical instrument. What a musical instrument produces goes far beyond what our common-sense expects from an ordinary object. Nevertheless, years of experience with instruments and music have provided perceptual models that correlate classes of gestures. Over time, a gesture vocabulary based on kinetic energy has thus been built up from these intuitive models. For example, a bowing gesture similar to the bow stroke on a violin suggests a continuous sound or a linear modification of a sound. A tap in the air suggests the attack of a percussive sound. A horizontal measuring sensor is assigned to a piano-like pitch change. Instrument-like gestures lead us to movements such as bowing, playing keys, etc. These are all musical-instrument-related gestures.

2. **Gestures Embody a Symbolic Action**

   The second type of movement conveys gestures related to physical reality. The gestures can be borrowed from our experience with objects from everyday life, such as stirring a pot, throwing something away, sweeping or mopping with a broom, or tapping out something. Again, we are still in the realm of object-related gestures. For example, in Pamela Z's *Typewriter Song*, the typing movements create the sound of an old typewriter. Her fingers tap the air and produce recognisable, realistic typing sounds with a carriage return sound when she pulls her right hand to the left. With an accelerator built into my glove, I can make a throw-away movement and sounds are symbolically thrown into space. The movement triggers a specific sound that is spatialised using Ambisonic. The effortful action and emotionality enhances the symbolic action. Stirring movements coupled with sound filters, granulations and other sound manipulations may conjure up the idea of stirring liquid in a pot. The expressive quality of movement is coupled with an extrinsic thread from our everyday life that supports a kind of "story".

3. **Metaphorical Gestures**

   The third type of gesture attribution moves away from object-related movements and links gestures to metaphorical ideas, which can also have emotional characteristics, such as shaking the whole body with excitement or wildly waving sounds around. Metaphorical gestures therefore also convey an expressive and theatrical expression.

4. **Gestures Sculpt Vocal Sound in Space**

   These gestures are geometric movements to occupy space in a particular way. For example, the movement can focus on a linear direction. The difference between these gestures and metaphorical gestures is that they do not necessarily have expressive meaning. The movement of the body does not focus on conveying a certain expressive meaning, but on shaping the sound in space, such as a circling arm movement leading to modifications of a filter and the volume. Additionally, the gesture makes the sound circle in three-dimensional ambisonic space. With geometric gestures, performers can connect the sculpting of sound with bodily sensations, where the inner felt-sense connects with the touch of the outer.

5. **Gestures as Choreographic Game**

   The fifth variant comprises all four surrogate gestures described above. Conceptually, the logically designed gestures are broken up and reinvented in a choreographic game. The nature of the gesture makes the audience unsure about the source and/or the cause of the gesture. We may not be sure how the sound is made to behave as it does. There are gestures which are related to the sonic outcome; or meta-movements, large geometric gestures, whole-body movements that can express metaphorical meanings. The performer's art lies in mastering the different gestures, and in being aware of the differences in the creation of meaning, as she or he goes back and forth between instrumental, symbolic, metaphorical and sound-sculpting gestures in a choreographic game.

4.4.9 Co-player Conclusions

The overriding feature of this dynamic framework is that the co-players are linked together in a network that is operational in binding these players to a central embodied and vocal meaning. The goal of this framework for meaning-making in gestural systems is to build an understanding of the way the levels interact with each other based on these different co-players. While maximum intensity in meaning-making integrates co-players into a single stream of a musical continuum, there are opposite situations where co-players break down into multiple streams that we can no longer hold together as a coherent piece.

Alex Nowitz says that, with the use of new musical interfaces, our duty is, to a certain degree, to provide an understanding of the overall instrument and to form the basis for an agreement to create meaning and thus communicate.

Embodied situations are felt or experienced with immediacy. For example, a piece might start with a cry and a dramatic gesture. The whole presence of the singer might be fearful. Her body transports a felt tension opening up to many possibilities for growth, enhancement of meaning, and development. The threatening characteristics of the situation take on new meaning as the music develops and as the singer engages in gesture and sound. Each stage of the piece's development opens up possibilities for further exploration of its fuller meaning. That will come only as the singer marks more distinctions, offers more connections and takes embodied action with, for example, fast and energetic gestures connected to immediate recordings of her cries. The desperate situation becomes more meaningful as the layers of the cry develop higher density in the relation of the embodied and the mediated voice and the kind of gesture interlinking the two realms. The situation may dissolve into an abstract realm as the cry develops into a sonic wall with lots of feedback and granulation. The meaning flips from the intrinsic qualities of the cry—who is crying and why— into a spectromorphological excitement of a sonic atmosphere with a specific colour. Each stage of an embodied situation's development opens up possibilities for further exploration of its fuller meaning, as the singer marks more distinctions, recognises more relations and connections and takes action.

"Electroacoustic music allows us to overcome certain biological, physical, and emotional limitations" (Hewitt 2006 in Mainsbridge 2022). As we saw in the second section, spectromorphological listening enables the overcoming of certain biological, physical and emotional meanings. The cry can transform the traditional feminine meaning of sound into a re-imagined identity. The disembodied voice offers a variability of persona references and thus expands the meaning of the given body, the voice. The kind of gestural quality or bodily presence that accompanies the sound of a cry can change its meaning in a communicative way. Johnson states that movement is one of the principal ways by which we learn the meaning of things and acquire our ever-growing sense of what our world is like:

> The key is that meaning is not just what is consciously entertained in acts of feeling and thought; instead, meaning reaches deep down into our corporeal encounter with the environment. The meanings must be grounded in our bodily connections with things, and they must be continuously "in the making" via our sensorimotor engagements (Johnson 2007).

How many layers can we focus on at the same time? Which aspect dominates which others? Are there signifiers and signifieds? In a stream of a continuum, we may focus on selective attention, divided attention and temporal aspects of attention.

> My attention, during the performance situation, is shifting from dance to sound, from vocal expression to the act of engineering, that is, live recording and playing back. The audience might not be able to see or detect that, but for me, it is clear how the different areas of vocal performance, movement, and technical aspects interact. For example, in order to focus on whole-body movements, I need to let go of the musical aspect for a tiny little moment. At the same time, the applied movement feeds back into the momentum of sound creation. The only way to master an interdisciplinary performance practice is to gradually shift the performer's attention from one to the other. Sometimes one needs to do things even simultaneously. However, we are human beings we cannot apply multitasking for too long of a period since it is extremely exhausting. Therefore we have to shift our attention and look after our

attention span for different tasks. To me, it is intriguing to have the opportunity of going back and forth between the vocal, the music-making, and the movement-related parts of a performance. The vocals are always between the body and the clone of the voice, between the dance and the manipulated sonic result. What I'm always coming back to, in this very complex performance situation, is my own live voice. This, maybe, is the main agreement between the audience and me (Nowitz 2022).

In this field of vibration, the embodied voice contributes and the networked assemblages of co-players to the functioning of nano-operations, of subjectivities that endlessly fragment and regroup through mediated voices whose imaginative potential produces new meanings.

The creation of meaning encompasses the entire relational field of the co-players, which is created by the presence of the vocalist with the gestural system.

Our capacity to grasp meanings, and our capacity for reasoning, depends on our conscious use of symbolic representations in the mind that somehow can relate to things outside the mind (Johnson 2007). Numerous scientific studies examining how meaning is transported when speaking have shown that facial expressions, gestures and body language disproportionately contribute to the understanding of the content. We perceive meaning in embodied ways. Meaning traffics in patterns, images, qualities, feelings, and eventually, in concepts and cognitive descriptive propositions. According to Merleau-Ponty (Merleau-Ponty 1999), the understanding of gestures is based on the mutual correspondence of my intentions and the other's gestures, my gestures and the intentions expressed by my behaviour. This inversion is based on the functionality of a common musical language that is understood by both performers and the audience. Based on our experiences with the voice's persona references, vocal images, gesture patterns and kinetic energy linked with sound, an embodied communication through gesture, expression and body presence allows new meanings.

Creating an agreement may foreground one of the co-players and set it in a specific relationship with the others. And with the next piece, the performer can introduce new relationships between gestures and sonic outcomes and change the meaning of the gestural instrument from an instrument to a body extension. Whether a specific gestural surrogacy, a communicative movement, or the expressive quality of a sensor's affordance foregrounds the game, the performer will always project a degree of human intention into the gestural system.

Understanding the potential of each player and levels of interaction in a gestural system supports meaning-making in sensor interface performance. Thus, multisensory connections between the embodied and disembodied voice in relation to the co-players clarify essential contexts in the interaction with the machine and make the listening experience a more extensive artistic experience within this frame of reference.

Embodied human–computer interaction finally means including the computer beyond its technical functions into our experiential world, be it as a counterpart with its calculative possibilities that surpass the human brain as well as in its bulkiness and the dangers of crashing. In an embodiment, I embrace, so to speak, all its possibilities and deficits and create new vocal body images through the composition of mapping strategies. Freedom here also means implementing new experiential images to the machine. What does it mean to play a sensor? What expressive qualities do I draw from this, and which of my embodiments in the performance do I allow myself to be surprised by?

As a singer, I am a human instrument, and I have a computer instrument. The re-incorporation of the electrified vocal phenomena through gestures reconnects the "outermost" with the "innermost". The disembodied voices, whether precomposed samples or directly modified vocal phenomena, invite re-embodiment by the vocalist through gestures, facial expressions and bodily presence. In the embodied human–machine interaction, I, as a singer, let worlds of experience emerge for the machine. A double bass remains a double bass, but I create new machine images in the human–machine exchange. What we see and hear is constantly renegotiated in the stream of musical events.

In an embodied practice, the computer becomes a body extension through gestural communication. I charge the space "in-between" me and the computer instrument with embodied expressivity and intentionality to make the machine a part of me. Pamela Z considers the entire system of human–computer interaction as her instrument:

> I consider the entire apparatus that is the combination of my voice and the processing of my voice as my instrument. When I am singing and processing my voice in real-time, it is very organic to me. It is not like something that I feel as artificial. And also, it does not feel like it is external or outside of me. It feels like it is all one unified part of what I am doing (Pamela Z 2021)

The relationship between me as a singer–performer and the computer–software is an imagined musical dialogue between human and machine: the computer interprets my input. It generates a response based on my programmed reaction patterns. Metaphorically speaking, the machine listens and responds to me according to predefined concepts. The whole system takes on the role of a co-player, whereby the computer's responses can, at best, simulate actions.

4.5 Outlook and Reflections

Designing and performing with gestural interfaces has uncovered a new hybrid practice for vocalists. As Marie Mainsbridge says:

> The unique experience of playing a gestural instrument, which only a small percentage of musicians experience, can prompt unique ways of experiencing music physically (Mainsbridge 2022).

We have seen that embodied engagement with sensor interfaces can expand vocal agency and establish a new organology within a system. The potential of interface performance to raise body awareness through further embodiments of sound with the machine is obvious. Engaging with such systems can lead to new creative discoveries, alter identities and expand movement and vocal vocabulary and skills. It requires a commitment to work out different modalities of the hybrid system: learning and exploring programs, composing content, practising singing, coping with technical crashes and finding new technical solutions, experimenting, practising, developing ideas, practising again and so on.

We are currently in the midst of a radical technological revolution with highly intelligent, autonomous computer systems that learn and also adapt to our behaviour (Brandtsegg 2020). New technological tools expand our applications of live electronics as machine learning not only adapts to our aesthetic imagination but can also generatively learn and save, for example, three-dimensional motion sequences in real-time. This may allow us to think further about body images in embodied performances and consider how we link humans with machines in musical performances. Interfaces with machine-learning capabilities can serve as an experimental and creative platform or laboratory for our embodied being-in-the-world with machines, how we act with our bodies in sound-worlds and how our voices create new body images. Vocalists playing with vocal abstractions, sometimes detached from gender, create innovative connections between action and sound liberated from traditional body images. They shape the behaviour of the gestural system by reframing old practices and forming new ones through the emergence of vocal worlds impregnated with new ideas and fluid body images.

Mainsbridge says of embodiment that the vocalists make the machines their own in new, highly individual ways:

> The voice and electronic devices are integrated and not separate like the singer-instrument accompaniment model. There is a fusion between instrument and body, unlike in any other type of performance practice (Mainsbridge 2022).

An embodied performance blurs the perception of control over the machine. It establishes a unique relationship between human and machine, in which performer and machine form a unity expressed in vocal sound and music.

Thinking about the co-players of the embodied vocabulary for gestural systems can help us understand ergomimetic principles, regardless of the different types of hardware and software used. It can help us break down outdated body images and contribute to culturally diverse designs for performers to create gestural systems appropriate for various body types and preferences. The valorisation of the tool and the focus on the equipment in live electronic music could risk a gendered divide. But if women, men and diverse beings design, compose and physically perform gestural systems, they are also responsible for the body images they create with them: "Designers need to envision an alternative future to replace outdated and dismantled social conventions" (Mainsbridge 2022).

This would then mean that we use artificial intelligence and creative mapping in such a way that performers invent new body–computer interactions through their imagination and a kinaesthetic sense that makes the intangible tangible through their bodily contribution to music-making. We are not moving towards a solid new practice. I rather feel that we are moving away from the predominance of linear concepts between movement and sound towards multiple new embodied human–computer interactions and inherent meanings waiting to be explored.

References

Baumann F (2010) Interfaces in der live-performance. In: Harenberg M, Daniel W (eds), *Klang (ohne) Körper*. Bielefeld, Transkript Verlag

Brandtsegg Ø (2020) An interface to an interface to an interface. ICLI Proceedings Trondheim

Damasio A (2003) Looking for Spinoza: joy, sorrow and the feeling brain. Harcourt, San Diego

Dourish P (2004) Where the action is: the foundations of embodied interaction. MIT Press, London

Gelineck S (2012) Doctoral thesis, Aalborg University. Exploratory and Creative Properties of Physical-Modeling-based Musical Instruments. https://vbn.aau.dk/files/316465627/Gelineck_Thesis.pdf, Accessed 12 Aug 2022

Gibson JJ (1986) The ecological approach to visual perception. Psychology Press, New York

Godøy RI (2006) Gestural-Sonorous objects: embodied extensions of Schaeffer's conceptual apparatus. Organised Sound 1(2): 149–57. https://doi.org/10.1017/S1355771806001439. Accessed 12 Aug 2022

Harenberg M (2010) Mediale Körper—Körper des Medialen. In: Harenberg M, Daniel W (eds) *Klang (ohne) Körper*. Bielefeld, Transkript Verlag

Hewitt DG (2006) Doctoral thesis, University of Western Sydney, Australia. Composition for Voice and Technology

Johnson M (2007) The meaning of the body: aesthetics of human understanding. University of Chicago Press, Chicago and London

Kim JH (2010) Embodiment musikalischer Praxis und Medialität des Musikinstruments—unter besonderer Berücksichtigung digitaler interaktiver Musikperformances. In Harenberg, Michael und Daniel Weissberg, *Klang (ohne) Körper*. Bielefeld, Transkript Verlag

Magnusson T (2019) Sonic writing, technologies of material, symbolic and signal inscriptions. Bloomsbury Academic, New York

Mainsbridge M (2022) Body as instrument: performing with gestural systems in live electronic music. Bloomsbury Academic, New York

Merleau-Ponty M (1999) Phenomenology of perception. Trans. Donald A. Landes. London, Routledge

Mudd T (2019) Material-oriented musical interaction. In: Holland S et al (eds) New directions in music and human–computer interaction. Cham, Springer, pp 123–133

Palombini C (1998) Technology and Pierre Schaeffer: Pierre Schaeffer's Arts-Relais, Walter Benjamin's technische Reproduzierbarkeit and Martin Heidegger's Ge-stell. Organised Sound 3(1):35–43. https://doi.org/10.1017/S1355771898009157, Accessed 11 Aug 2022

Schubert A (2021) Switching Worlds. Wolke Verlag, Hofheim am Taunus

Tanaka A (2019) Embodied musical interaction. In: Holland S et al (eds) New directions in music and human–computer interaction. Cham, Springer, 135–154

Verstraete P (2015) Die Demaskierung der körperlosen Stimme: Eine sozio-ästhetische Betrachtung interaktiver Bewegungs-Musik, https://www.academia.edu/11159726/Die_Demaskierung_der_k%C3%B6rperlosen_Stimme_Eine_sozio_%C3%A4sthetische_Betrachtung_interaktiver_Bewegungs_Musik, Accessed 12 Aug 2022

Wechsler R (2006) Artistic considerations in the use of motion tracking with live performers: a practical guide. In: Broadhurst S, Machon J (eds) Performance and technology. London, Palgrave Macmillan, pp 60–77. https://doi.org/10.1057/9780230288157_5, Accessed 11 Aug 2022

Windsor WL (2011) Gestures in music-making: action, information and perception. In: Gritten A, King E (eds) New perspectives on music and gesture. Ashgate, Farnham, pp 45–66

Full interviews

Norderval K (2021) Interview. http://www.franziskabaumann.ch/en/press/interview3-norderval.php, Accessed Aug 2022

Nowitz A (2021) Interview. http://www.franziskabaumann.ch/en/press/interview2-nowitz.php, Accessed 12 Aug 2022

Pamela Z (2021) Interview. http://www.franziskabaumann.ch/en/press/interview1-pamela.php, Accessed Aug 2022

Tanaka A (2022) Interview. http://www.franziskabaumann.ch/en/press/interview4-nowitz.php, Accessed Aug 2022

Printed in the United States
by Baker & Taylor Publisher Services